The High Life: Communication with the Holy Spirit

Chris A. Legebow

Copyright © 2018 Chris A. Legebow

All rights reserved.

ISBN: 978-1-988914-10-7

DEDICATION

After my salvation, I began to hear God's voice clearly. After the Baptism of the Holy Spirit, I began to obey the Holy Spirit's promptings and became a willing servant to obey God. It is my prayer, you will give your life fresh to God as a willing servant who clearly hears the voice of God.

CONTENTS

	Acknowledgments	i
1	The Holy Spirit Speaking	1
2	Conversations with God	16
3	Communion with God	38
4	The Altar	81
5	Old Covenant	89
6	Living by Faith	100
7	Prophetic prayer and declaration	110
8	The engrafted word	119
	Conclusion	131
	Prayers	138

ACKNOWLEDGMENTS

All scripture taken from Biblegateway.com
Modern English Version (MEV)

1 THE HOLY SPIRIT SPEAKING

Prayer – Holy Spirit – living – God speaking to you

This book on prayer is different than my first book on kinds of prayer. It is rather a practical, more personal teaching on intimate communion with God. Once a person becomes a Christian, a whole new life of opportunity comes to him or her. The Scriptures describe it as being translated from darkness to light. It is not simply a comparison. It is a reality. The spirit of a person who does not know God is like a dry, shrivelled fruit or vegetable. It has no quality of spiritual life within it. Man's spirit was meant to be filled with the presence of God. The Holy Spirit comes to live within the human spirit as a person receives Jesus Christ as Saviour. It is hard to explain without making analogies because there is nothing quite like it. The Holy Spirit of God literally comes within the shrivelled spirit of a person and fills the spirit so it is lively, alert, full of life, joy, peace. That is simply a symbol of the miracle of the new birth.

Colossians 1: 13 He has delivered us from the power of darkness and has transferred us into the kingdom of His dear Son, 14 in whom we have redemption through His blood, the forgiveness of sins.

A new Christian will begin to view the world completely differently because with God living on the inside of him or her, man begins to view things from a godly perspective rather than just a fleshly human perspective. The spiritual truths of God become revelation to the Christian; the Christian sacraments and the covenants become clear and sure signs of God's love towards man. There will be a desire in the person for more of God. It is a yearning to pray, praise, read the Bible, Study the Bible, be with other Christians in worship. Also, there will be a development of spiritual fruit on the inner most parts of the person. He or she will start being transformed by God from glory to glory by God's Spirit from the inside of the person.

2 Corinthians 3: 18 But we all, seeing the glory of the Lord with unveiled faces, as in a mirror, are being transformed into the same image from glory to glory by the Spirit of the Lord.

Literally by being in the presence of God 's Holy Spirit– in praise and prayer and communion, a person is changed. Just as Moses who went on Mount Sinai to get God's Commandments returned to the camp with his countenance shinning the glory of God so that He put a veil on his face because people were staring at him.

Exodus 34: 29 When Moses came down from Mount Sinai with the two tablets of testimony in the hands of Moses, when he came down from the mountain, Moses did not know that the skin of his face shone while he talked with Him. 30 So when Aaron and all the children of Israel saw Moses, amazingly, the skin of his face shone, and they were afraid to come near him. 31 But Moses called to them, and Aaron and all the rulers of the congregation returned to him, and Moses spoke to them. 32 Afterward all the children of Israel drew near, and he commanded them all that the Lord had spoken to him on Mount Sinai, our spirits glow with the light of the Holy Spirit after we have been in prayer or praise. The people around him feared Moses because of the light of God.

The response of a person not right with God is to keep distance from God. A person who desires God more than anything, will press in to God knowing that God whose bright light of holiness shines on us, can also transform us so that our spirits, our human soul is literally changed to be more like God. Rather than fear God knowing we are not perfect, we run to God so that He might change us. There is no fear; there is such love and desire for God the person presses in to God with all his or her being.

Exodus 34: 33 When Moses finished speaking with them, he put a veil over his face. 34 But whenever Moses went in before the Lord to speak with Him, he took the veil off until he came out. Then he came out and spoke to the children of Israel what he had been commanded. 35 The children of Israel saw the face of Moses, that the skin of Moses' face shone, and then Moses put the veil over his face again until he went in to speak with Him.

Moses had over 40 years of communion with God before that day he came from Mt. Sinai shinning with the glory of God. The more we are in the presence of God, the more we will know God's overwhelming love; we will feel the comfort of His Holy Spirit and receive directly from God's Spirit speaking to our spirit.

Praying God's Word can build your faith

Talking to God in prayer can be spoken or it can be silently prayed with the will. I like using my voice to speak to God because my own ears can hear my prayers and I can praise and worship as I pray. It strengthens the inner man. Faith comes by hearing God's Word. Often, I pray using the scriptures as a guide, because praying God's Word is directly agreeing with God.

There have been occasions in my profession as a teacher that I left teaching notes for a substitute teacher because I was selected to write curriculum. To the non – teacher, it means I was creating writing curriculum for my school, but also had to write lessons for whoever might take my place in the classroom. The teacher could with authority speak to my class my direct will or plan for the class because he or she had my notes. Most often those who followed the teaching notes, did well. Similarly, it is true with God's Word. If we directly use God's Words to pray, we are directly speaking to Him what is already His will towards us, so it is coming into agreement with what God has already promised us.

Prayer is spirit to Spirit communing with God

There have been occasions where a spoken prayer was not possible, such as in a public place as in my job. A silent prayer, quick or not is effective if it is prayed with faith. The important thing to realize is that prayer is spirit speaking to God's Holy Spirit. Jesus is the intercessor. Immediately as we pray, God hears us. Often those silent prayers or quick prayers yield quick results also. Because the Holy Spirit is with us always, we can always commune with God. We don't have to be in a certain place or doing particular things – God is always with us. Some of my short prayers are prayers of "God help me to find the item." Afterwards, I give a short prayer of thanks.

The way to pray

My book on Kinds of prayer can give practical tips on different types of prayers. This book is to emphasize the person's one on one relationship with the Holy Spirit. Although I will mention different aspects of kinds or prayers, it is not the focus of teaching. The focus is on relationship; rather than talk about God as a far-off deity that we connect with, through a system of techniques, God, The Holy Spirit, is a person who is living on the innermost parts of believers. Christians can develop their relationship with God so that their lives are pleasing to God; they will live holy lives because they are abiding in God's presence. The important part is that if we are living in the constant presence of God, God can use us to do His will in the earth. We can literally be the Body of Christ helping people in the earth because we are not continuously praying to just make it to heaven. Please forgive my bluntness. A person cannot wholly desire God with all his or her heart, soul mind and strength and also pursue sin passionately. They do not coexist. They cannot coexist. Sin and righteousness are different spiritual destinations. Just as a person cannot physically travel to Russia and to

Columbia simultaneously, a person must choose which direction he or she desires to go.

Galatians 5: 25 If we live in the Spirit, let us also walk in the Spirit. 26 Let us not be conceited, provoking one another and envying one another.

Areas of vulnerability – weak spots – must pray the word of God – dress in spiritual armour – rely on Jesus Christ's righteousness not our own.

Spirit and truth

The only way to communicate with God is to do it in spirit and truth. If it is not sincere, it is just words that are uttered. If it is not true worship, we will know and of course God will know. There is no sense in trying to fool God because He knows everything about you. God sees the heart. God knows the very thoughts and intensions of your heart. Those who truly desire God will draw unto Him truly with all their being.

John 4: 23 Yet the hour is coming, and is now here, when the true worshippers will worship the Father in spirit and truth. For the Father seeks such to worship Him. 24 God is Spirit, and those who worship Him must worship Him in spirit and truth."

Romans 14: 22 The faith that you have, have as your own conviction before God. Happy is he who does not condemn himself in what he approves. 23 But he who doubts is condemned if he eats, because it is not from faith, for whatever is not from faith is sin.

Hebrews 4: 12 For the word of God is alive, and active, and sharper than any two-edged sword, piercing even to the division of soul and spirit, of joints and marrow, and able to judge the thoughts and intents of the heart. 13 There is no creature that is not revealed in His sight, for all things are bare and exposed to the eyes of Him to whom we must give account.

Wholly Holy

Giving yourself wholly occurs at salvation but it should continue every day of your life throughout all your life.

1 Thessalonians 5: 23 May the very God of peace sanctify you completely. And I pray to God that your whole spirit, soul, and body be preserved blameless unto the coming of our Lord Jesus Christ. 24 Faithful is He who calls you, who also will do it.

Each day of your life, you've got an opportunity to give yourself unto God. Each day of your life, you get a new opportunity to live unto God. Receive the day with an embrace, thanking God for it. Give yourself as a living sacrifice to God. That means, you choose God first. It means you praise and worship Him. It means you read the Word of God. It means you pray and express love towards Him. As He speaks to you, you obey Him.

Romans 12: 1 I urge you therefore, brothers, by the mercies of God, that you present your bodies as a living sacrifice, holy, and acceptable to God, which is your reasonable service of worship. 2 Do not be conformed to this world, but be transformed by the renewing of your mind, that you may prove what is the good and acceptable and perfect will of God.

Keep God first

It is a relationship of communion. It is loving God with your life. We get 24 hours a day. What we choose to do with our priorities determines the type of people we are; pursuing God first will be reflected in our activities and planning of our day. Scheduling prayer with God should be the most important aspect of a Christian's life. I know that in our fast-paced society words such as these make people reply they don't have enough time to truly pursue God. The truth is, you could get up earlier. You could turn the tv off and go and pray. You could do one less leisure activity and read your Bible. It really is our choice. In this modern society, many people watch television as a hobby rather than for entertainment only.

There is a lie that many people believe and that is that prayer is a duty. People believe that they do it as it earns them points with God or makes them righteous. These are lies. The truth prayer is communion. It is joyful. It is exciting. It is fascinating. It is overwhelming joy if you are truly connecting with God. Prayer is communication directly with the Holy Spirit. God's Spirit directly communes with our human spirit. I mean we become as one with God. God lives in us and through us. He is a person who is fascinating and exciting. Once you pray and know that God hears your prayers and answers you, speaks to you and communes with you, you will want to talk to God throughout your day, as the Apostle Paul encouraged us to pray without ceasing.

God living in you

Knowing that God is with you always is a comfort like no other. Being given to prayer means your heart is pure and you are ready for God to direct you or lead you in any way. Yes, we do our earthly duties such as work and family, but God is living in us and through it as we do it. That means God can speak to us, inspire us, quicken us or give us special words to speak to someone. Being a living member of the Body of Christ is like being on a team that is always ready to obey. It is sort of like being in the army where you are on call 24 hours a day. God can use you should you yield your life to Him throughout the day. The Holy Spirit will use you in your life and in your career and in your family and relationships and community etc. It is not an isolation from society. There are certainly occasions for person set apart time with God, but God wants to use you as an agent of righteousness on the earth. It will involve all aspects of your life.

May God reveal to you the awesomeness of being a Christian. Jesus Christ's Holy presence is living within us. Just as the Holy presence of God was in the ark of the covenant with Moses, We are as the ark of the covenant – The Holy Spirit lives within us – His Holy presence. The part that is different is that we are living willful creatures and God can use us to be agents of righteousness. We can help people, serve, pray, give, encourage etc.

2 Corinthians 4: 6 For God, who commanded the light to shine out of darkness, has shone in our hearts to give the light of the knowledge of the glory of God in the face of Jesus Christ.

7 But we have this treasure in earthen vessels, the excellency of the power being from God and not from ourselves.

God's angels surround us. They protect us as the angels carved on the ark of the covenant spread their wings over the mercy seat on the top of it. God is with us always. It is a constant joy. It brings a peace that goes beyond all earthly definition. There is confidence knowing God is with you.

My point is that God will use you in your life: your career, your family, your personal life, your community. You are a member of the body of Christ in all those places; God is with you. God can give you inspired words to encourage someone or use you to pray for someone. It may be overtly or covertly. Just as there are soldiers in the army that are gathered together for strategic missions, there are other soldiers who are as secret agents who no one knows about but are there to help the mission succeed; we too will have opportunities to speak with people, pray for them etc. We will also have opportunity to privately pray for people and do God's will without anyone but God knowing about it.

The High Life

Not as a hypocrite

In fact, we are not to boast about our missions. Just as secret agents cannot brag about their secret missions to save lives, we are not to brag about our missions on earth. There is no room for pride or self-righteousness. We are simply agents of righteousness; God gets all the glory. Being able to receive missions from God, obey Him and keep our hearts pure without pride are essential if God is going to use us. Bragging about being God's servant is pride. Obeying God and giving God glory is Christian service. It is living in the high calling of your life.

Luke 18: 11 The Pharisee stood and prayed these things about himself, 'God, I thank You that I am not like other men: extortioners, unjust, adulterers, or even like this tax collector. 12 I fast twice a week, and I tithe of all that I earn.'

13 "But the tax collector, standing at a distance, would not even lift his eyes to heaven, but struck his chest, saying, 'God, be merciful to me a sinner.'

14 "I tell you, this man went down to his house justified rather than the other. For everyone who exalts himself will be humbled, and he who humbles himself will be exalted."

God is searching throughout the earth for people he can entrust with missions. I am sure we do not always know the importance of these missions. Simply speaking words of encouragement could literally help save lives. Simply giving in obedience to God could answer someone's prayer. Our obedience to the promptings of the Holy Spirit not only have earthly consequences, but also eternal reverberations. Just as a pond ripples wave after a stone is tossed into it, our words and actions on earth ripple throughout eternity. Being obedient to the Holy Spirit is essential.

God is seeking for those who will be wholly committed to Him so that we may do the will of God on the earth. God can use angels, but He most often chooses to use members of the body of Christ.

Isaiah 6: 8 Also I heard the voice of the Lord saying, "Whom shall I send, and who will go for us?"

Then I said, "Here am I. Send me."

It is the servant heart of Isaiah who gives his life to serve God by speaking the words God gives him. It is the same type of radical surrender that true Christians gladly do each day. We say yes to God each day. We offer ourselves so that God may use us to speak, to do, to pray etc. We are co laborers with God. We are coworkers with God. There is no higher call than to give you life as a living agent for Jesus Christ. Sometimes, it means sharing Christ with those who don't know Him. Sometimes, it means speaking words of encouragement to Christians. Often. it means private silent prayer but could sometimes be ministering prayer to a person.

1 Corinthians 3: 9 For we are laborers together with God: You are God's vineyard; you are God's building.

Humility is an essential character quality if we are to be successful and true ministers of Christ. Humility is a character quality we should all desire. Jesus is the example of humility as he came God as man and lived in our midst as one of us. He did not brag about the healings or miracles. He gave God all the glory. Pray asking God to reveal and correct any false motives. The Holy Spirit will do it. He will convict us or correct Him should we give ourselves to Him. A simple prayer to pray regularly is asking the Holy Spirit to be our senior partner. The term I get from Pastor Yonggi Cho's book of the same title. In the Holy Spirit my senior partner, he talks about surrendering to the Holy Spirit's leadings and promptings each day as a way of living in the Spirit and doing the will of God.

Worship privately as well as publicly

What we do in secret, God often rewards us openly for. The saint who prays every day alone, without anyone but God knowing, is earnestly serving the LORD as much as any public minister or preacher. Prayer alone should be most important to each Christian. Corporate prayer is also important, but God will often speak to you in your private prayer life to encourage you or a word to encourage others in the corporate prayer meetings.

Matthew 6: 5 "When you pray, you shall not be like the hypocrites. For they love to pray standing in the synagogues and on the street corners that they may be seen by men. Truly I say to you, they have their reward. 6 But you, when you pray, enter your closet, and when you have shut your door, pray to your Father who is in secret. And your Father who sees in secret will reward you openly.

Like a sporting event

I played organized sports most of my life. I like the activity; I like the training' I Like winning. As an athlete, I know that daily decisions to do repetitive exercises to strengthen and build strength and perfect skills is necessary to compete. There are special tournaments and events, but if there is no training, the person will do his or her best – but the winners or those who place high are those who do the daily training. I have known discipline in training and the joys of winning. I also know when I haven't trained as I should and how its affected my performance. Even if I placed highly, I knew it wasn't my best. Part of being an athlete, is trying to compete with myself by continuous self - improvement.

I give you this analogy of sport because many people have had some involvement with organized sports. A Christian could start praying for faith to raise the dead at the moment of the need. However, it would be wise to start praying it before a need arises. The Christian should be praying daily, stirring up his or her faith long before there is a situation. The person should become sensitive to hearing God's voice so that he or she can directly know how to pray the will of God and speak by faith the will of God in such a situation. Such an example can be found in Jesus healing the epileptic boy.

Matthew 17: 15 "Lord, have mercy on my son, for he is an epileptic and suffers terribly. He often falls into the fire and often into the water. 16 I brought him to Your disciples, but they could not heal him."

17 Then Jesus answered, "O faithless and perverse generation, how long shall I be with you? How long shall I bear with you? Bring him here to Me." 18 Jesus rebuked the demon, and he came out of him. And the child was healed instantly.

19 Then the disciples came to Jesus privately and said, "Why could we not cast him out?"

20 Jesus said to them, "Because of your unbelief. For truly I say to you, if you have faith as a grain of mustard seed, you will say to this mountain, 'Move from here to there,' and it will move. And nothing will be impossible for you. 21 But this kind does not go out except by prayer and fasting."

In this story, Jesus asserts faith by rebuking unbelief. He commands the demon to come out of the boy. The child is instantly healed because Jesus cast out the demon. The disciples were constantly with Jesus day and night. They heard his teaching. They healed others. They wanted to know why they could not heal the boy. Jesus explained that it was because of prayer and fasting. His answer is not talking about that one day. Jesus lived his life given to prayer and fasting. He was used to a lifestyle of connection with God. He knew that he had authority to rebuke the demon and heal the boy.

Feed your faith

Faith only comes by hearing the Word of God and hearing it over again. Romans 10: 17. It doesn't just mean hearing with your physical ears. It of course involves auditory but also receiving it in your spirit – listening to the Holy Spirit in the Scripture you hear more than words; you know the authority of the scripture because of your study and because God has revealed it to you. As you acknowledge God's Word as final authority and speak it and use it, you will have boldness to speak the Word of God expecting miracles to occur. Also, your listening to the Holy Spirit and speaking with Him gives you boldness to know you always have access to God.

Hebrews 4: 16 Let us then come with confidence to the throne of grace, that we may obtain mercy and find grace to help in time of need.

You will know that God hears you. You won't be trying to find a way to get God's ear, because you will be used to conversing with Him every day. You will have boldness not in your own righteousness, but in the righteousness of God imparted unto you. You will have boldness because you will realize that you are God's agent of righteousness in that situation. It is Jesus living in you in the person of The Holy Spirit that gives you boldness.

1 John 5: 14 This is the confidence that we have in Him, that if we ask anything according to His will, He hears us. 15 So if we know that He hears whatever we ask, we know that we have whatever we asked of Him.

Build up yourself so you can help others

Pray building up your faith daily with scriptures, praying them and confessing them until they become a part of you. Being filled with the Holy Spirit is the sure way to live in the supernatural. It is possible that you can be God's person in the scene at the exact moment someone needs a miracle. Be ready always. SEMPER PARATUS. It means you are always on guard for God. You are never off duty. In the army, we became one with our rifle. Everywhere I went, the rifle went. It could not be left unguarded. We were constantly commanded to care for it and to carry it every place. We were threatened that if it were lost, we would have to pay for it –

thousands of dollars. In the same way, a Christian should be with his or her Bible. It should accompany you always – on the inside of you as well as a copy either physical or digital that you could use to encourage someone with.

First, the Word of God is to build up yourself and encourage yourself. Next, it is to sow into others' lives to bring salvation, healing, deliverance, miracles, encouragement. God's Word in you with the faith of Jesus Christ who lives in you gives you boldness to help people.

Hebrew 4: 12 For the word of God is alive, and active, and sharper than any two-edged sword, piercing even to the division of soul and spirit, of joints and marrow, and able to judge the thoughts and intents of the heart.

As you are in communion with God living with Him is exciting. It may be that you pray with people in unusual places such as a restaurant or supermarket. It may be that you've got a Rhema Word from God that is living in you and the exact people who need that exact word come in proximity to you in the bank or in a store. It certainly means God will use you. The more you are communing with God, the more you can give.

You will feel a strong urge to give. It will become primary. You will be doing your ordinary life things, most excellently. If you fail, you will try again a different way. You will pray, knowing God will help you. You will also be on assignment for any type of situation. God can use angels and He does. Most of us do not know all the things angels protect us from or how they help us. God most often though likes to use people. God uses ordinary people like you or I who wholly give themselves to God and believe the Word of God and live it. God uses us to be his hands and feet in the earth. He will speak a word or prompt you to help others.

Pray for opportunities for God to use you

Many occasions of my life I encountered life changing moments with God at altar calls I would literally pray the words "O God use me". And what would happen on the way home is I would meet someone at a gas station or a store who I would speak with to encourage. There were occasions God gave me words of wisdom or words of knowledge about the people I met at a place and never saw again. I know that if God can use Balaam's donkey to speak, he can use me. I know that if God can use me, He can use anyone. It involves giving your life daily. It isn't a hobby or an aspect of your life. Living in the spirit is the life and what we do for others is a joy that comes from living in the Spirit.

Pray for yourself. Pray for your family spouse or children

Pray for yourself every day. Pray thanking God for your salvation, healing and deliverance. Just as the Israelites were taught to pray thanks for being rescued from slavery out of Egypt – and today their dependents continue to pray those prayers, we also should thank God for what He has done for us. We should also ask God to supply all our needs. He already knows them, but He does command us to ask of Him that He might supply.

John 15: 7 If you remain in Me, and My words remain in you, you will ask whatever you desire, and it shall be done for you.

Intercession: Pray for others

Praying for others is a privilege. You will know when you are to do it because God will quicken you to believe it is necessary. I remember myself learning this truth as I was a new Christian as God began to prompt me to pray for people around me in church and for those who had prayer requests in the service. I recognized it was important. People would greet me and ask me to pray for them. Sometimes, I forgot and then realized it shouldn't be left to memory. At first, I started jotting people's names in my Bible. Afterwards, it became so crowded with names, I wrote them in a book. Often when someone would ask for prayer, I would at that moment pray with him or her, so I would not forget. Often, God would place individuals on my heart and I began keeping a prayer list of people to pray for regularly.

James 5: 15 And the prayer of faith will save the sick, and the Lord will raise him up. And if he has committed any sins, he will be forgiven. 16 Confess your faults to one another and pray for one another, that you may be healed. The effective, fervent prayer of a righteous man accomplishes much.

The Holy Spirit will quicken to you your place in intercessory prayer. He will nudge you in your spirit and you will know you should pray for people, animals, situations etc. You will feel an impression in your spirit that causes you to know it is God. Pray for people and situations that directly affect your life. There is no end to the things you could be praying about. Not everyone has the same calling in prayer. Some pray over certain things constantly. Not all have the same calling as intercessors. In my role as a teacher, I see people differently than I would a carpenter or plumber or clerk. Each person has a realm or sphere of authority. It is important that we obey God and pray to impact our spheres of authority. It means that God can use you in an area I may never know and visa versa.

Some ideas for prayer you may not have considered

Pray for ministers of the gospel to remain strong and effective.
Pray for rulers in authority.
Pray for those people effected by world events.
Pray for God's will to do done in the earth.
Literally pray that God would release people to share Christ throughout the earth.
Pray for animals and that we would be wise stewards of the earth.
Pray for nations.
Literally all places on earth, all people on earth, all aspects of human life are aspects that can be impacted by prayer.

Pray for Godly Christian Character

Christian Character

The character of a Christian should be positive, optimistic, prayerful, believing God and living as though we believe it by our words, thoughts and deeds. It is commanded of us.

Philippians 4: 4 Rejoice in the Lord always. Again, I will say, rejoice! 5 Let everyone come to know your gentleness. The Lord is at hand. 6 Be anxious for nothing, but in everything, by prayer and supplication with gratitude, make your requests known to God. 7 And the peace of God, which surpasses all understanding, will protect your hearts and minds through Christ Jesus.

Praying God's Word over people is a sure way of aligning your prayers with God.

NOTE: Please if you are a new Christian or you have need of deliverance from addiction or bondage or healing, do not let my words impact you negatively. I would not have the boldness to state it if Jesus were not able to completely take any person and revolutionize his or her life so that it could be true. If you need deliverance or healing, I highly recommend my book on Jesus: Saviour, Healer, LORD. I would also not deter you from praying for others now. You do not have to be perfect to pray for others; you only need to be obedient and willing.

If you are not sure how to pray for people, begin by praying a scripture over the people. Pray for God to reveal to you how to pray. Also, pray in tongues. As you pray in the Spirit, the Holy Spirit is praying through you the perfect will of God.

Romans 8: 26 Likewise, the Spirit helps us in our weaknesses, for we do not know what to pray for as we ought, but the Spirit Himself intercedes for us with groanings too deep for words. 27 He who searches the hearts knows what the mind of the Spirit is, because He intercedes for the saints according to the will of God.

Praying for yourself should include Spiritual growth. Literally pray the fruit of the Spirit for yourself. Pray that God will develop these fruit in your character. Reading and acknowledging it is not enough. Pray that God will change you from glory to glory.

Galatians 5: 22 But the fruit of the Spirit is love, joy, peace, patience, gentleness, goodness, faith, 23 meekness, and self-control; against such there is no law. 24 Those who are Christ's have crucified the flesh with its passions and lusts. 25 If we live in the Spirit, let us also walk in the Spirit.

The development of Spiritual fruit is necessary for us to be true Christians or followers of Christ. It is not something a person can do with willpower, although you must yield your will to God, so He can transform you. It is not by copying others that you can get it, although having true mentors can impact your life and lead to Spiritual growth. Only the Holy Spirit can transform you so that true godly character is developed in you. God's word expresses His will towards us. By reading, praying and confessing the Word of God, the Word of God becomes so much a part of you that there is no difference between you and the Word of God. It is that ingrafted word that is able to transform the soul.

James 1: 21 Therefore lay aside all filthiness and remaining wickedness and receive with meekness the engrafted word, which is able to save your souls.

Some of the most radical life transformations occur as you pray asking God to change you or you respond to an altar call, giving more of yourself or a different aspect of your life to God. You will not necessarily know it as it is an inward miracle and often is not known or recognized until God reveals it afterwards. It becomes part of our living witness or our testimony that we can share to build faith in others.

End of chapter questions

1. Clearly identify an occurrence of God speaking to you in some way. Explain it and how it affected you.
2. If God has spoken to you in more than one way give a brief telling of each of the occurrences.
3. Examine your own spiritual life. Consider areas of your life that you can eliminate or reduce so that you can communicate with God through Bible study, prayer, worship.
4. Write a strategy to get more of God's word in you.

2 CONVERSATIONS WITH GOD

CHAPTER 2

1 Thessalonians 5: 16 Rejoice always. 17 Pray without ceasing. 18 In everything give thanks, for this is the will of God in Christ Jesus concerning you.

Prayer is conversation with God. As soon as you become a Christian, you will know the presence of God's Holy Spirit living within you. Your spirit speaks with God directly. It is supernaturally normal for a Christian to speak to God throughout the day and throughout the evening. You may be talking to God quietly as you mow the lawn or do construction. It is a way of coming to God recognizing that life on earth is an assignment for you as an ambassador for God. I am talking about doing chores or manual type jobs.

What you think about most determines your direction. Should you be thinking of God, talking to God about ordinary things, God will commune with you. Often, I ask God to help me find solutions to normal things in my day. The request is quick but sincere and true. God can give us insight beyond all earthly insight. Not only can He help us do ordinary things, God can use us to do excellently rather than almost excellent. Invite God into every part of your life. Praying without ceasing is not repetitive prayer. I am talking about having a posture of prayer and receptivity to God throughout your day.

We don't only worship God in a certain place. Because we are the temple of the Holy Spirit, God is always with us. Jesus made the way for us so that we could live in the presence of God through his blood. Relying on God to help us, is a way of honouring God. It is also the way of an exciting life.

2 Corinthians 5: 18 All this is from God, who has reconciled us to Himself through Jesus Christ and has given to us the ministry of reconciliation, 19 that is, that God was in Christ reconciling the world to Himself, not counting their sins against them, and has entrusted to us the message of reconciliation. 20 So we are ambassadors for Christ, as though God were pleading through us. We implore you in Christ's stead: Be reconciled to God. 21 God made Him who knew no sin to be sin for us, that we might become the righteousness of God in Him.

Hebrews 10: 19 Therefore, brothers, we have confidence to enter the Most Holy Place by the blood of Jesus, 20 by a new and living way that He has opened for us through the veil, that is to say, His flesh, 21 and since we have a High Priest over the house of God, 22 let us draw near with a true heart in full assurance of faith, having our hearts sprinkled to cleanse them from an evil conscience, and our bodies washed with pure water. 23 Let us firmly hold the profession of our faith without wavering, for He who promised is faithful

Conversations with God

Conversations with God are like conversations with your closet friend or most intimate companion. You can pray the scriptures in a more formal type setting or you can pray a prayer list during your regular prayer. I am not saying there is never a formal way of coming to God. Conversations with God can also be as a person would speak to a companion. God cares about what you like and what you don't like. God cares about all aspects of your being. There are moments that there is silence and only the presence of God is there to comfort you and strengthen you. There are also less formal types of discussions with God about yourself or others.

In prayer, it isn't your eloquence with words that God likes. If you are simply saying words believing you will be earning points with God, it is as nothing. Should you be doing some type of manual work, and you can sense God's presence, lean in to Him as you would towards a friend who beckons you to come closer. You may get some revelation about yourself; you may be prompted to pray for someone or visit someone. You may get revelation about your work itself.

The Apostle Peter

On one occasion, Peter and John were on their way to worship God at the Temple, when they saw a lame man who was begging. It was in the ordinary aspect of life. Something tugged at the Apostle's heart and he knew that it was that lame man's day for healing. By faith the apostle told the man to rise up and be healed in the name of Jesus. The man obeyed and was completely healed. It brought a miracle to that man's life. It brought glory to God. It was part of the normal supernatural life the disciples had with Jesus. I am saying, God wants everyone of us to live in the realm of the supernaturally normal.

Acts 3: 1 Now Peter and John went up together to the temple at the ninth hour, the hour of prayer. 2 A man lame from birth was being carried, whom people placed daily at the gate of the temple called Beautiful to ask alms from those who entered the temple. 3 Seeing Peter and John about to go into the temple, he asked for alms. 4 Peter, gazing at him with John, said, "Look at us." 5 So he paid attention to them, expecting to receive something from them.

6 Then Peter said, "I have no silver and gold, but I give you what I have. In the name of Jesus Christ of Nazareth, rise up and walk." 7 He took him by the right hand and raised him up. Immediately his feet and ankles were strengthened. 8 Jumping up, he stood and walked and entered the temple with them, walking and jumping and praising God. 9 All the people saw him walking and praising God. 10 They knew that it was he who sat for alms at the Beautiful Gate of the temple. And they were filled with wonder and amazement at what happened to him.

The Apostle Peter was doing his regular praying and worshipping one day when God showed him a vision. It had significance for that very day but also for all of the Gentile people including me and possibly you. God revealed to Him something profound in the vision. He did not completely understand it until he preached to Gentiles and they received the baptism of the Holy Spirit. People who once never knew God, were saved and received not only their salvation but the baptism of the Holy Spirit.

Apostle Peter

Acts 10: 9 The next day as they went on their journey and drew near the city, Peter went up on the housetop to pray about the sixth hour. 10 He became very hungry and desired to eat. But while they prepared a meal, he fell into a trance 11 and saw heaven opened, and a vessel like a great sheet, tied at the four corners, descending to him, and let down to the earth. 12 In it were all kinds of four-footed animals of the earth and wild beasts and reptiles and birds of the air. 13 Then a voice came to him, "Rise, Peter; kill and eat."

14 Peter said, "Not at all, Lord. For I have never eaten anything that is common or unclean."

15 The voice spoke to him a second time: "What God has cleansed, do not call common."

16 This happened three times. And again the vessel was taken up into heaven.

The High Life

The only way to live a supernaturally normal life is to yield yourself daily to God and follow the prompting of the Holy Spirit.

Prayer

It can occur anywhere. It can be instant. It can be short. Short prayers are just as important as long prayers should you be truly praying.

Pray daily – petitions and requests as well as praying for wisdom and discernment.

Pray for others: Intercession but also pray that God would use you throughout your day. You don't have to remember each of these things as a study. As you press into God with all your being, these types of conversations with God will arise out of your spirit.

Scripture

As you memorize scripture – say it and pray it – it will help you to learn but it will also benefit you strengthening you and becoming life to you.

Pray scriptures over yourself that God might let His word impact your spheres of authority.

God may speak during your regular prayer with Him. Praying regularly should be a pleasure of a Christian. Joy of communion with God. Express your joy with the psalms or other passages of scripture. Read them to God. Pray them as you read them.

Psalm 16: 9 Therefore my heart is glad, and my glory rejoices;
   my flesh also will rest in security.
10 For You will not leave my soul in Sheol,
   nor will You suffer Your godly one to see corruption.
11 You will make known to me the path of life;
   in Your presence is fullness of joy;
   at Your right hand there are pleasures for evermore.

Psalm 9: 1 I will give thanks to You, O Lord, with my whole heart;
   I will declare all Your marvelous works.

Psalm 9: 2 I will be glad and rejoice in You;
   I will sing praise to Your name, O Most High.

God is in the midst as you pray and worship.

Psalm 22: 3 But You are holy,
   O You who inhabits the praises of Israel.
4 Our fathers trusted in You;
   they trusted, and You did deliver them.

Planned prayer

   Choose a duration if necessary time yourself so you can pray. It is helpful to create a prayer list. You can type people to pray for, things you are praying for, salvation requests, healing requests, special miracles, answers to prayer. Kind of organize your prayers by putting them on paper – the main points. It will help you as you pray. Each day you may use it as a guide but not be confined by it. New things that come to you, pray and include. There will be events or world news you will want to include. A new believer should choose a duration. It may be 15 minutes. Don't simply wander about in your prayers. Write the main points on paper. As you are growing in your relationship with God, you will pray more.

   Larry Lea, an American Evangelist write a book Tarry with me an Hour. He talks about praying the LORD's prayer in that book. He writes a chapter on each aspect of the LORD's prayer and shows how people can use it as an outline for prayer. It is an excellent book. There are all different kinds of prayer and all kinds of occasions to pray. My book on Kinds of Prayer: knowing them and using them goes into much detail on the different kinds of prayer. I only mention here that prayer is not necessarily the same each day. There will be different things you pray for even though there will be some things the same.

   Reading about people who wrote on prayer is helpful. Pastor Yoggi Chou of Korea talks about praying different kinds of specific prayer and how God taught him to pray specific prayers to get specific results. Smith Wigglesworth was a mighty Apostle of faith, who did not go more than 30 minutes without talking about God or praying. God used him in the working of miracles. There are unknown women and men, teenagers and children who pray in their private lives that directly impact the earth because of their sincerity and faith.

   As you would with a friend, develop your prayer life with God. It starts with you – create a list. If necessary time yourself so you can do it and do the other stuff in your day. Be sure to include thanksgiving, praise and worship. Those things draw you closer to God because you magnify Him rather than yourself.

Psalm 100 describes a kind of progression of prayer. First was the outer court where there were many people. Priests offered sacrifices to God there. Many people praised God and received encouragement in the outer court. The next place was the Holy place. In it Levitical priests offered incense to God as commanded by Moses. Only the Levitical priests could go in there. Jesus made the way into that Holy place accessible to all who would believe that he died for their sins and received salvation. We can praise God in the Holy place. It is a normal place of praising God and enjoying His presence. Often in congregations on Sundays people gather and sing praises together in the sanctuary. The place is made Holy by the living presence of God there. You can also enter the Holy place by singing praises to God in your private place whether it be home or even in your car.

Psalm 100: 4 Enter into His gates with thanksgiving,
   and into His courts with praise;
   be thankful to Him, and bless His name.
5 For the Lord is good; His mercy endures forever,
   and His faithfulness to all generations.

Finally, there is a place of the innermost sanctuary of the Temple – it is the Holy of Holies. It is the place the Ark of the covenant was kept. It had the real presence of God in it. The presence of God was revered and honoured. Only the high priest could enter that place and it was only to atone for the sins of the people by pouring blood on the mercy seat atop the ark of the Covenant. Jesus gave us entrance into the Holy of Holies by His blood. We can directly speak to God. God has miraculously made a way to connect with us through the blood of Jesus so that we can have intimacy with God. Only Jesus can give us this special gift and it can not be earned or purchased.

There are many Christians who praise God in the sanctuary or outer court. There are some Christians who press in and enter the Holy place with God by their seeking God daily in prayer and praying for others. They may praise God throughout the day. Often, they get a song of worship in their spirits throughout the day. They may sing them out loud or they may simply keep praising God within.

The Holy of Holies is the place where you yield yourself completely to

God as an offering. It is a place of total abandon. You yield to God's Spirit without limit. You most often don't talk or praise here. Often you worship silently or fall to your knees of prostrate or sing in tongues. It is a place of worship. There is no higher pleasure than being in God's ultimate Holy presence.

Suggested Guide for new believers or those wanting to improve their prayer life

Thanks – Start your prayer with thanking God. Starting with thanksgiving immediately gets you off your mind. You begin magnifying God and what He has done. Thank Him for the people in your life. Thank Him for your home. Thank Him for your job. Thank Him for your salvation. Truly mean it. What it does is magnify God and your spirit focuses on God.

Praise – Praise is offering songs to God. You can start by singing some worship choruses from church or from your worship CD's. You can start singing the new song of the LORD. What the new song is referring to is your own individual thanksgiving and praise to God in your own words. It is not a script. You start praising God for what He's done for you. Start praising God for His mercy towards you etc. Let the words flow. Sing in English and sing in tongues. If you have not received the Baptism of the Holy Spirit yet, the good news is you can. Please see the prayer at the end of the book on how to pray for the Baptism of the Holy Spirit.

Once you have been baptized with the Holy Spirit speaking in other tongues, it should be part of your prayer language. You should be praising God in tongues. God gave you the language to use. It is not for goosebumps or entertainment. The baptism of the Holy Spirit empowers you to serve God. The baptism of the Holy Spirit is God's Spirit praising through your spirit.

Petition – make your petitions known. Pray your important points on your prayer list. It will differ each day. You will emphasize somethings more one day than another. God hears your prayers. You will know that God has heard you as sure as you know your friend has heard you in a conversation. In the natural you see your friend nodding his head; he may respond with words; he may ask a question. You know the person has heard you. You can be that sure that God has heard you also as long as your prayers line up with scripture.

God will never contradict His word. That means if you are praying anything that violates a person's free will or breaks the laws of God or the laws of your land, you are asking amiss. It means that God will not give you things outside of His will for you. For example, praying that some person will love you and marry you is violating a person's free will. You should preface that type of prayer with God please bless so and so. If possible, let that person come into my life.

Avoid soulish (unscriptural) selfish prayers. Never violate someone's human will.

Confess Scripture/pray scripture

An excellent way to start a prayer life is by learning scriptures and praying the scriptures. Learning the scriptures is important because you will know what God's will is. You will learn what pleases Him and what He hates. You will be able to pray more effectively because you will know God more. Praying scripture is you coming into agreement with what God's will is. It helps get the word of God on the innermost part of your spirit – memorizing scripture improves your prayer life. Memorizing scripture improves your life: physically, your soul life (mind, will and emotions) your relationships and family, and of course your spiritual life. The more you get God's Word into you in the innermost parts, the more you become like God. The more the Holy Spirit can quicken those scriptures to you. It is a direct dialogue with God. You align your words with God's Word, miracles begin to manifest.

2 Timothy 3: 16 All Scripture is inspired by God and is profitable for teaching, for reproof, for correction, and for instruction in righteousness, 17 that the man of God may be complete, thoroughly equipped for every good work.

Joshua 1: 6 "Be strong and courageous, for you shall provide the land that I swore to their fathers to give them as an inheritance for this people. 7 Be strong and very courageous, in order to act carefully in accordance with all the law that My servant Moses commanded you. Do not turn aside from it to the right or the left, so that you may succeed wherever you go. 8 This Book of the Law must not depart from your mouth. Meditate on it day and night so that you may act carefully according to all that is written in it. For then you will make your way successful, and you will be wise. 9 Have not I commanded you? Be strong and courageous. Do not be afraid or dismayed, for the Lord your God is with you wherever you go."

Worship – after you have made your prayer requests and prayed scriptures over yourself and loved ones, praise and worship God. You can either sing some choruses or sing the new song of the LORD; most certainly, you should be praising and worshipping in truth. You must truly be sincere with God. As you truly worship God, you will feel His Holy presence. You will feel yourself giving all of yourself to God as a living sacrifice. You will be adoring God. You will not simply be magnifying Him you will be overwhelmed by His Holy presence. Always remember it is only because of Jesus that you and I have this awesome privilege.

I personally must praise God afterwards and express thanksgiving once more that God inhabits me. You may be different. It would be good to express thanks and go about the rest of your day.

You should always have a private prayer life even if you pray with your spouse or your family or your church each day. It is essential that you yourself have a connection with God.

Purpose in yourself that you desire to draw close to God everyday. There may be days you are able to spend long in the presence of God. Enjoy your relationship.

How to draw close

Draw near unto me and I will draw near unto you...

You can literally pray the scriptures that God will draw near unto you because you are drawing unto Him. You can literally pray "God I am seeking you with all my being." You can pray for God to be magnified. Literally start praying " I magnify you O God." As you pray the scriptures with faith, God's Holy presence manifests.

James 4: 8 Draw near to God, and He will draw near to you. Cleanse your hands, you sinners, and purify your hearts, you double-minded.

Jeremiah 29: 12 Then you shall call upon Me, and you shall come and pray to Me, and I will listen to you. 13 You shall seek Me and find Me, when you shall search for Me with all your heart. 14 I will be found by you, says the Lord, and I will turn away your captivity and gather you from all the nations and from all the places where I have driven you, says the Lord, and I will bring you back into the place from where I caused you to be carried away captive.

Jesus is the righteousness of God. He is living in you in the presence of the Holy Spirit. Your relationship with God is completely and wholly because of Jesus Christ. Meekness, humility should be your heart attitude. If you feel any sense of pride because of your prayer life, it is carnal. It is not of God. A true Christian knows Jesus is the only way to righteousness. Jesus is the only way to God. It is not by any other means but because of your faith in Jesus Christ.

Colossians 1: 19 For it pleased the Father that in Him all fullness should dwell, 20 and to reconcile all things to Himself by Him, having made peace through the blood of His cross, by Him, I say—whether they are things in earth, or things in heaven.

Ephesians 2: 8 For by grace you have been saved through faith, and this is not of yourselves It is the gift of God, 9 not of works, so that no one should boast.

Prayer – start by talking to God. Praising Him and honouring Him. Pray the scriptures.

Ask Seek and Knock

Matthew 7: 7 "Ask and it will be given to you; seek and you will find; knock and it will be opened to you. 8 For everyone who asks receives, and he who seeks finds, and to him who knocks, it will be opened

There are three types of prayers in the above scripture. Asking of God your prayer requests.

Seeking God – drawing close to God. Purposing in your human will to turn towards God. Seeking God – prayer with listening – worship, praise, ask God to speak to you to be magnified in your life and to give you wisdom or revelation.

I didn't know much about the knocking until I heard Marilyn Hickey's teaching on it. It became so clear to me that I knew it was an insight that should be shared.

Knocking is something you do to enter a new space. In the spirit also, there are doors of opportunity and there are doors of utterance, doors of authority. You may spiritually see a door, or you may just sense it. You will know there is a new opportunity. It will be knowledge in your spirit. You will know the right thing to do is to knock. So literally pray. "God. I knock on the door of utterance that is will be opened unto me." Pray for discernment on the type of door that it is. Pray literally positioning yourself to knock expecting God to answer you with a new opportunity. God can do it. It's a type of prayer. The prayer of knocking to go through a door of opportunity.

Learning God's Voice

You will learn God's voice by being in His presence often. Read the Word of God. It is God's direct will for all humans and life for all of mankind. There are scriptures of things that occurred and things that yet shall occur. The Bible is God's clear word for people.

It is important to have a friend you can pray a prayer of agreement with. That person should totally be in agreement with you concerning the thing you are praying about. God teaches us that if any two or more agree in prayer about something, He will answer. It is not instead of private prayer. It is in addition. It strengthens the prayer. I believe there are angels released in direct answer to prayer. He sends angels to answer prayer as we pray.

Matthew 18: 19 "Again I say to you, that if two of you agree on earth about anything they ask, it will be done for them by My Father who is in heaven. 20 For where two or three are assembled in My name, there I am in their midst."

Hebrews 1: 14 Are they not all ministering spirits sent out to minister to those who will inherit salvation?

Believe the truth and that is that once God has heard your prayer, the answer is on the way. God will release angels to bring it to pass.

Once you grasp the truth that God and His Word are inseparable, God is one with His Word. He does not lie; you will begin reading God's Word as though it directly applies to you because it does. You will begin seeing God's Word as a direct message towards you about how to live your life. Once the Holy Spirit quickens the scriptures to you, you will never settle for anything less than God's best for your life. Once you know it is God's will to prosper you with health, strength, long life, prosperity, you will begin to read the scriptures prayerfully. You will desire more of God's Word. The Word brings revelation of God's character, His will, His plan. You will desire God's Word as a person might desire natural bread. It is ordinary; it is part of our life, but it is also most excellent when you desire it. It becomes special. God's word is our daily bread.

Matthew 4: 4 But He answered, "It is written, 'Man shall not live by bread alone, but by every word that proceeds out of the mouth of God.'[a]"

The Gospel of John is not only beautiful poetry, but it is especially beautiful because it is truth. Jesus is the Word of God. Jesus is the Living word of God. It is mentioned in this passage of scripture and again by Jesus himself. Jesus and the Word of God are one.

John 1: 1 In the beginning was the Word, and the Word was with God, and the Word was God. 2 He was in the beginning with God. 3 All things were created through Him, and without Him nothing was created that was created. 4 In Him was life, and the life was the light of mankind. 5 The light shines in darkness, but the darkness has not overcome it.

6 There was a man sent from God whose name was John. 7 This man came as a witness in order to testify concerning the Light, that all men through Him might believe. 8 He was not this Light, but was sent in order to testify concerning the Light.

9 The true Light, which enlightens everyone, was coming into the world. 10 He was in the world, and the world was created through Him, yet the world did not know Him. 11 He came to His own, and His own people did not receive Him. 12 Yet to all who received Him, He gave the power to become sons of God, to those who believed in His name, 13 who were born not of blood, nor of the will of the flesh, nor of the will of man, but of God.

14 The Word became flesh and dwelt among us, and we saw His glory, the glory as the only Son of the Father, full of grace and truth.

Jesus the living bread

John 6: 51 I am the living bread which came down from heaven. If anyone eats of this bread, he will live forever. The bread which I shall give for the life of the world is My flesh." 53 Jesus said to them, "Truly, truly I say to you, unless you eat the flesh of the Son of Man and drink His blood, you have no life in you. 54 Whoever eats My flesh and drinks My blood has eternal life. And I will raise him up on the last day. 55 For My flesh is food indeed, and My blood is drink indeed. 56 Whoever eats My flesh and drinks My blood remains in Me, and I in him. 57 As the living Father sent Me, and I live because of the Father, so whoever feeds on Me also will live because of Me. 58 This is the bread which came down from heaven, not as your fathers ate manna and died. He who eats this bread will live forever."

Jesus is referring to Himself as the living bread, the sacrifice offered once and for all people. Jesus is referring to Himself as the manna that is to be our daily bread as God provided manna (the bread from heaven- literally - what is it) for Israel for forty years. Jesus is referring to the Passover supper where the cup of salvation was taken and the cup of covenant with God. He is that cup. Jesus is referring to the covenant of the New Testament of His life given for us for eternity. Jesus and His Word are one.

As you are praying regularly, God may quicken a scripture to you. That means it will come to you and you will realize God is speaking to you.

DISCERNING GOD'S VOICE

Once you have prayed and receive God's Word, pray about it. Search the scriptures. Pray. Ask God to reveal to you how to apply it in your life. Pry for God to give you revelation concerning it.

1. Pray that you can discern that God is speaking to you.
2. As you know God is speaking, listen with all your being.
3. Pray – receive it as Mary received revelation from the angel.

Luke 1: 30 But the angel said to her, "Do not be afraid, Mary, for you have found favor with God. 31 Listen, you will conceive in your womb and bear a Son and shall call His name JESUS. 32 He will be great and will be called the Son of the Highest. And the Lord God will give Him the throne of His father David, 33 and He will reign over the house of Jacob forever. And of His kingdom there will be no end."

34 Then Mary said to the angel, "How can this be, since I do not know a man?"

35 The angel answered her, "The Holy Spirit will come upon you, and the power of the Highest will overshadow you. Therefore, the Holy One who will be born will be called the Son of God. 36 Listen, your cousin Elizabeth has also conceived a son in her old age. And this is the sixth month with her who was declared barren. 37 For with God nothing will be impossible."

38 Mary said, "I am the servant of the Lord. May it be unto me according to your word." Then the angel departed from her.

Embrace the Word

Once The Holy Spirit quickens a scripture to you or speaks a word to you, pray for its meaning to be made clear to you. Pray that you might have wisdom to know it and how to apply it in your life. It may mean a new way of perceiving something. It may mean obedience to something. It can release all sorts of potential to you that can totally bless your life. Kenneth Copeland has a whole series of books called One Word from God can totally transform your......The truth is one word from God can totally change each aspect of your life.

I have realized and am still constantly realizing something: God is eternal. Once God speaks a word to you, it is for all of your life long. It can be applied to many different aspects of your life. Often you are to share those truths with others and to speak the word, teach the word and write the word. It may mean writing a journal or diary. It may be publishing a book. It may be imparting the word into a Bible class. It certainly is for you and most often it is also for you to share with all the people who can receive spiritual things from you. Not all people want to know about things of the spirit. Those who do want to know the things of God are important, and we should share what God has spoken to us to others.

Timothy 2: 2 Share the things that you have heard from me in the presence of many witnesses with faithful men who will be able to teach others also.

Attitude

A believer's attitude at receiving the word of God should be similar to receiving a treasure. The Word of God is like dynamite. It can produce mighty results. The scripture describes it:

Hebrews 4: 12 For the word of God is alive, and active, and sharper than any two-edged sword, piercing even to the division of soul and spirit, of joints and marrow, and able to judge the thoughts and intents of the heart.

Quick and alive are not just adjectives. The word is quick as a living thing is quick. Alive is living. The Word of God is alive. It is living. It can produce results because it is God's presence in the essence of the words. Just as a sharp sword can carefully divide between joints and marrow, the word of God can divide soul from spirit and truth from lies. God's word is eternal. One word from God is for all of your life long. Often you are to share it with others as a testimony or write it or teach it to your children or family. Even if you do not understand it, you embrace the word and pray for revelation. An example of it is seen with Mary, the mother of Jesus.

Mary received God's Word

Mary received the word and came into agreement with it. It was a prophetic word about her destiny. She embraced it although most certainly she didn't understand all the aspects of it.

Pray about it asking God for revelation. I mean literally pray "O Holy Spirit give me revelation. Show me. Direct me. Show me how to apply it in my life."

Obey the Word – If you know you have heard from God – obey him. If He asks you to do something, diligently do it. If it is something you don't understand, do everything you can to get understanding. Most importantly ask the Holy Spirit to direct you and guide you to the answers.

God may speak to tell us to get rid of stuff.

As the Apostle Preached at Ephesus, the people were convicted and became Christians. By their own conviction, they burned all their occult books.

Acts 19: 17 This became known to all Jews and Greeks living in Ephesus. And fear fell on them all, and the name of the Lord Jesus was magnified. 18 Many who believed came confessing and telling their deeds. 19 Many who practiced magic brought their books together and burned them before everyone. They calculated their value, which equaled fifty thousand drachmas.[a] 20 So the word of the Lord powerfully grew and spread.

God might speak to have us contact someone to encourage him or her. Philip and the Ethiopian Eunuch. God specifically sent him to a particular person so that he could be saved and bring the truth of Jesus Christ to Ethiopia.

Acts 8: 26 Now an angel of the Lord said to Philip, "Rise up and go toward the south on the way that goes down from Jerusalem to Gaza." This is desert. 27 So he rose up and went. And there was a man of Ethiopia, a eunuch of great authority under Candace, queen of the Ethiopians, who was in command of her entire treasury. He had come to Jerusalem to worship. 28 He was returning, sitting in his chariot and reading the book of Isaiah the prophet. 29 The Spirit said to Philip, "Go to this chariot and stay with it."

God may bring you revelation of Scripture

People were impacted by reading of God's word as it was restored to them. One of my favourite passages of scripture is in Nehemiah where the people rejoice at receiving God's word. They had been captive. They had gone without hearing God's words for years. After the walls were built around Jerusalem, the Temple was restored, and Nehemiah had the scriptures read to all the people who gathered on a day of celebration. The people stood for hours listening to God's word being read. They wept at the beauty of it and because they knew they had not been obeying it and with excitement because of it being restored. The scripture reveals the people's joy at being renewed by God's presence and deep respect for the scriptures.

Nehemiah 8: 1 All the people gathered together as one man in the area in front of the Water Gate, and they asked Ezra the scribe to bring the Book of the Law of Moses, which the Lord had commanded to Israel.

2 On the first day of the seventh month, Ezra the priest brought the Law before the congregation of men, women, and all who could listen with understanding. 3 In the area in front of the Water Gate, he read aloud from sunrise until midday to the men, women, and those who could understand. All the people listened attentively to the Book of the Law.

4 Ezra the scribe stood on a raised wood platform, which they had made for the purpose. Beside him stood Mattithiah, Shema, Anaiah, Uriah, Hilkiah, and Maaseiah on his right hand; and on his left hand, Pedaiah, Mishael, Malkijah, Hashum, Hashbaddanah, Zechariah, and Meshullam.

5 Ezra opened the book in the sight of all the people (because he was above all the people), and, as he opened it, all the people stood up. 6 When Ezra blessed the Lord as the great God, all the people responded "Amen, Amen!" By lifting up their hands as they bowed their heads, they worshipped the Lord with their faces to the ground.

7 Then Jeshua, Bani, Sherebiah, Jamin, Akkub, Shabbethai, Hodiah, Maaseiah, Kelita, Azariah, Jozabad, Hanan, Pelaiah, and the Levites, explained the Law to the people while the people stood in their place. 8 They read from the book, from the Law of God, with interpretation, and they gave the sense, so that the people understood the reading.

9 Then Nehemiah the magistrate, Ezra the priest and scribe, and the Levites

who were teaching the people said to all the people, "This day is holy to the Lord your God. Stop mourning and weeping." (This was because all the people wept when they heard the words of the Law.)

10 Then he said to them, "Go your way. Eat the fat, drink the sweet drink, and send portions to those for whom nothing is prepared; for this day is holy to our Lord. Do not be grieved, for the joy of the Lord is your strength."

11 So the Levites quieted all the people, saying, "Hush! Because today is holy you should stop being so sorrowful."

12 Then all the people went to eat, to drink, to send portions, and to enjoy a great celebration because they had understood the words declared to them.

Ezra and Nehemiah got Israel that was gathered to rejoice rather than weep. They had a party celebrating God's presence and his Word.

God's Word is always prophetic

Because God's word is alive, because God's word has within itself the power to bring itself to come to pass, it is always prophetic. That is why the word of God never returns void. Should we sow the word of God into our own lives or into others lives, it always produces results. Because it is as seed, it always produces after its kind. Just as carrot seed produces carrots, the word of God produces spiritual results.

Isaiah 55: 11 so shall My word be that goes forth from My mouth;
  it shall not return to Me void,
but it shall accomplish that which I please,
  and it shall prosper in the thing for which I sent it.

God's word has significance not only in the physical realm but also in the spiritual.
You should sow and keep sowing

Should you sow the word of God into your life regularly through reading the scriptures, praying the scriptures and confessing them, God will quicken those scriptures to you with revelation and understanding. The more of God's word you sow, the more you will be strengthened in your spirit and the more God will use the word of God to speak to you. It's not magic. It's Jehovah. God keeps his word. His word is eternal. His word is his will towards us.

If you know The Holy Spirit has clearly spoken a word to you, and you pray and get understanding of it, you should share it with people God places in your path. God will reveal the correct people. Don't simply share precious things with just anyone. Share them with the people God prompts you to share them with. There are occasions that God speaks to you and it is only for your life. It is important, but it doesn't apply to anyone else. There are words you get from God that you speak to your friends and family. There are words you get from God and you know you are to speak them to certain people only.

2 Timothy 2: 2 Share the things that you have heard from me in the presence of many witnesses with faithful men who will be able to teach others also.

God will confirm

John 14: 27 Peace I leave with you. My peace I give to you. Not as the world gives do I give to you. Let not your heart be troubled, neither let it be afraid.

The Holy Spirit abiding in us will give us peace when something is in alignment with God's word and God's will. God might speak to give us a confirmation of direction – peace the umpire through the Holy Spirit.

If you do not know what God wants you to do in a situation and you have earnestly prayed, seek God for confirmation. Say what you plan to do based on your knowledge and wisdom and the Word of God. Rather than do nothing, start in a direction. God can steer you once you start in a direction.

God never contradicts His Word

Psalm 119: 89 Forever, O Lord, Your word
   is established in heaven.

If it is a prophetic word about your destiny, your spirit will acknowledge it. It will never contradict the word of God. It will never violate the will of a person. God will not tell you to marry someone who is already married. God will never contradict scripture. The commandments are the plumb line of God's Word. That means any other word you get from God will always agree with it. It means that you should use scripture are a measuring line to align your life. If you know there is an area of your life that does not align with God's word, repent and obey God's Word. The Holy Spirit will prompt you and bring conviction. The Holy Spirit will never condemn you. Usually words about your destiny give you promptings on heart attitude and godly character. It's a call to a higher life. It's a call to give more of yourself to God. It usually is like a spiritual promotion from God. If there is no peace in it, it is not a word from God.

Philippians 4: 4 Rejoice in the Lord always. Again. I will say, rejoice! 5 Let everyone come to know your gentleness. The Lord is at hand. 6 Be anxious for nothing, but in everything, by prayer and supplication with gratitude, make your requests known to God. 7 And the peace of God, which surpasses all understanding, will protect your hearts and minds through Christ Jesus

Even when the Apostle Paul knew (by God telling him) that he would become a prisoner and be beaten and abused, he willingly and peacefully accepted the word. He had complete peace because he knew he was in the will of God. He knew he must preach to certain people.

Acts 20: 22 "Now, compelled by the Spirit, I am going to Jerusalem, not knowing what shall befall me there, 23 except that the Holy Spirit testifies to me in every city that imprisonment and afflictions await me. 24 But none of these things deter me. Nor do I count my life of value to myself, so that I may joyfully finish my course and the ministry which I have received from the Lord Jesus, to testify to the gospel of the grace of God.

Even when the apostle was taken in chains by the Roman soldiers to be judged by Caesar, and the ship he was on was in a terrible storm and it was for many days, Paul had peace and was able to speak peace to the people on the ship including the Romans.

Acts 27: 21 After they had long abstained from food, Paul stood in their midst and said, "Men, you should have listened to me and not have set sail from Crete, incurring this injury and loss. 22 But now I advise you to take courage, for there will be no loss of life among you, but only of the ship. 23 For there stood by me this night the angel of God to whom I belong and whom I serve, 24 saying, 'Do not be afraid, Paul. You must stand before Caesar. And, look! God has given you all those who sail with you.' 25 Therefore, men, take courage, for I believe God that it will be exactly as it was told to me. 26 Nevertheless, we must be shipwrecked on a certain island."

Only God can speak to a person to strengthen and to give peace such as in these instances. There are so many such examples. Daniel had peace in the lion's Den (Daniel 6: 21-22) Hananiah, Azariah and Misael, had peace as they were thrown in the furnace.

Daniel 3: 16 Shadrach, Meshach, and Abednego answered and said to the king, "O Nebuchadnezzar, we do not need to give you an answer in this matter. 17 If it be so, our God whom we serve is able to deliver us from the burning fiery furnace, and He will deliver us out of your hand, O king. 18 But even if He does not, be it known to you, O king, that we will not serve your gods, nor worship the golden image which you have set up."

It is God's Holy Presence that brings peace to a believer that is a peace beyond all human comprehension. Only God can do it.

Receive the Word

Receiving the Word is essential. Aligning yourself with the word is important. If you know that God has spoken to you, but you disobey, you will not know peace until you obey. Should God speak to you and you disobey, it is a sin. An example is Jonah who tried to run from God. He was in direct disobedience to God. He joined with men going to Joppa and a terrible storm arose because of Jonah. Jonah knew the storm was because of him. He asked the people to throw him overboard into the sea. They did it and the storm ceased. Jonah was swallowed by a whale.

Jonah 1: Now the word of the Lord came to Jonah son of Amittai, saying, 2 "Get up, go to Nineveh, the great city, and cry out against it, because their wickedness has come up before Me."

3 But Jonah got up to flee to Tarshish from the presence of the Lord. He went down to Joppa and found there a ship going to Tarshish. He paid its fare and went down into it to go with them to Tarshish from the presence of the Lord.

As Jonah prayed earnestly, God answered his prayer.

Jonah 2:
9 But I will sacrifice to You
   with the voice of thanksgiving;
I will pay what I have vowed.
   Salvation is of the Lord!"

10 Then the Lord spoke to the fish, and it vomited Jonah out upon dry land.

Once more God commanded Jonah to go prophesy to all of Nineveh. Jonah obeyed.

Should God speak to you, you should immediately obey. God will never speak to you as entertainment. Should he speak to you to speak to someone or to give to someone, it is a matter of eternal priority to God. You have been given a gift and the way of receiving the gift is to obey. Surely you will be blessed by obeying. The message following is especially the confirmation of the prophet Ezekiel's calling but it can apply to anyone God has spoken a message to reach other people.

If you speak the message to the ones God sent you to, you will be considered innocent, even if they do not obey. If you do not warn the people or speak the message, you are responsible to God for your disobedience and you are guilty of not speaking to that person.

Ezekiel 33: 2 Son of man, speak to the children of your people and say to them: If I bring a sword upon a land, and the people of the land take a man from among them and set him for their watchman, 3 and he sees the sword come upon the land and blows the trumpet and warns the people, 4 then whoever hears the sound of the trumpet and does not take warning, and a sword comes and takes him away, his blood shall be upon his own head. 5 He heard the sound of the trumpet yet did not take warning. His blood shall be upon himself. But he who takes warning delivers his soul. 6 But if the watchman sees the sword come and does not blow the trumpet and the people are not warned and a sword comes and takes a person from among them, he is taken away in his iniquity. But his blood I will require from the hand of the watchman.

Chapter 2
End of chapter questions

1. If you have received a RHEMA word or revelation from God, explain how it came and also your reaction to it.
2. Explain how you learned to discern hearing God's voice.
3. Consider praying for family or friends with scripture expecting God to cause them to draw closer to God

3 COMMUNIION WITH GOD

Chapter 3

Communication with God is made possible because of Jesus atonement in dying for our sins. Faith in Jesus death, burial and resurrections, makes it possible for the Holy Spirit to live inside of you. The resident Holy Spirit communicates with our human spirit constantly. A Christian is never alone. The Holy Spirit is a constant companion. I acknowledge Jesus as LORD of my life through willfully giving the Holy Spirit authority in each area of my life. It means I know that only the Holy Spirit can empower me to live a godly Christian life. Because the Holy Spirit is so gentle, so caring, and because God's Holiness is quite different than our soulish lives, we must learn to discern the voice of God speaking to us. He may speak to us in different ways. The Holy Spirit will never contradict God's written Word because He is the author. He teaches us, leads us and guides us. Even though the Holy Spirit may speak to us to do something, we must submit our human will to God.

Colossians 1: 27 To them God would make known what is the glorious riches of this mystery among the nations. It is Christ in you, the hope of glory,

Learning to discern: Completely relying on the Holy Spirit

One of most important things to a Christian, besides knowing that God has saved you and that you are forgiven is learning to recognize God is speaking to you. Discerning of spirits is an important gift to pray for yourself and for every new Christian. Only in recognizing God's voice from any other makes it possible for you to obey God and live for Him. Samuel was a special child in that he was an answer to prayer to his barren mother. She vowed to God that she would dedicate him and give him to God to live for him. She kept her vow. As soon as he was weaned, she brought him to the temple and gave him to Samuel as an offering unto God. Samuel only saw his family when they came to temple to worship. He lived as a member of the priesthood. Eli the priest raised him. He learned all things that had to do with being a servant of God.

The following passage reveals how Samuel came to learn God's voice.

1 Samuel 3: 4 Then the Lord called to Samuel, and he answered, "Here I am." 5 He ran to Eli and said, "Here I am, for you called to me."

And he said, "I did not call. Return, lie down again." And he went and lay down.

6 The Lord called Samuel again. So Samuel arose and went to Eli, and said, "Here I am, for you called me."

And he answered, "I did not call, my son. Return, lie down again."

7 Now Samuel did not yet know the Lord, nor had the word of the Lord been revealed to him.

8 The Lord again called Samuel a third time. So he arose and went to Eli and said, "Here I am, for you called me."

Then Eli understood that the Lord was calling to the boy. 9 Therefore Eli said to Samuel, "Go, lie down And it will be, if He calls you, that you will say, 'Speak, Lord, for Your servant listens.' " So Samuel went and lay down in his place.

10 The Lord came and stood, and He called as at other times, "Samuel, Samuel."

Then Samuel said, "Speak, for Your servant listens."

The pattern

Because Samuel answered God by giving himself to listen, God spoke to him. The voice that spoke to Samuel was familiar. He thought it must have been Eli. The voice of the LORD spoke repeatedly to get Samuel to listen. The voice of God spoke prophetically to Samuel so that he may know the things that would occur. Hearing from God was important not only that one day but for all of the days of his life. Because Samuel lived as a holy priest and prophet of God serving God and caring for people all of his life, he had to know the voice of God to pray for people and to give words of wisdom to people. The first important thing to do is pray that God give you discernment to know his voice. Literally pray "God give me discerning of spirits strong so that I can know your voice and obey you."

Accept the word

Hearing the voice of God always confirms the scriptures, never contradicts the scriptures. There are people in the Bible who heard the word of God but disobeyed God. Accepting the words God speaks to you are also necessary as obedience is required.

Jonah 1: 1 Now the word of the Lord came to Jonah son of Amittai, saying, 2 "Get up, go to Nineveh, the great city, and cry out against it, because their wickedness has come up before Me."

God spoke to Jonah and told him to go prophesy repentance to the people of Nineveh because God was surely going to punish them if them didn't repent. Jonah knew it was God speaking to him. Jonah understood that God's judgement was going to be on Nineveh, yet he didn't obey. He chose to go in the opposite direction. His attempt to escape God was foolish but also selfish. There is no way a person can escape God. His attempt to do it only shows that he didn't understand how magnificent and omnipotent God is. Also, it is selfish. Jonah reveals later that his reason for running away from Nineveh is because he knew God would be merciful and that if the people repented, God would forgive them. Jonah did finally go and preach repentance and the king, and all the people and animals of Nineveh repented and fasted and prayed. God forgave them. Rather than be joyful, Jonah was angry at God's mercy towards sinners.

Jonah 4: 1 Now this greatly displeased Jonah, and he became angry. 2 He prayed to the Lord and said, "O Lord! Is this not what I said while I was still in my own land? This is the reason that I fled before to Tarshish, because I knew that You are a gracious God and merciful, slow to anger, abundant in faithfulness, and ready to relent from punishment. 3 Therefore, Lord, take my life from me, for it is better for me to die than to live."

3 But Jonah got up to flee to Tarshish from the presence of the Lord. He went down to Joppa and found there a ship going to Tarshish. He paid its fare and went down into it to go with them to Tarshish from the presence of the Lord.

Jonah did not have godly compassion on sinners. He was more concerned about his reputation as a prophet than people's eternal souls. Jonah was certainly imperfect, yet God chose him to go prophesy a word that brought salvation to the whole town and spared them from judgement. Obeying the word of God is important but also heart attitude is important. A person used by God should pray for godly character and mercy towards people. If for no other reason, God uses Jonah to show us He can use any person. Once you have heard from God, obey God with a pure heart – one without malice or hatred.

Pray that you align with the word as Mary did

Mary was approximately age 14 when God sent the angel Gabriel to speak to her. The Bible does not tell us that Mary was praying for a special miracle or anything. Suddenly an angel appeared to her and instructed her that she would give birth to the Saviour Jesus. She was a believer. She knew an angel from God was speaking to her. She knew that the message was naturally impossible. I don't think she knew the implications of the words. I don't believe she understood how it would all occur. Mary understood it was a special calling. She knew it was from God. She said yes even though she didn't comprehend it. She agreed to the word with her human will by saying " let it me to me as you have said". It means although her human self did not understand, she accepted God's special prophetic word to her.

Luke 1: 26 In the sixth month the angel Gabriel was sent from God to a city of Galilee named Nazareth, 27 to a virgin betrothed to a man whose name was Joseph, of the house of David. And the virgin's name was Mary. 28 The angel came to her and said, "Greetings, you who are highly favored. The Lord is with you. Blessed are you among women."
29 When she saw him, she was troubled by his words, and considered in her mind what kind of greeting this might be. 30 But the angel said to her, "Do not be afraid, Mary, for you have found favor with God. 31 Listen, you will conceive in your womb and bear a Son and shall call His name JESUS. 32 He will be great, and will be called the Son of the Highest. And the Lord God will give Him the throne of His father David, 33 and He will reign over the house of Jacob forever. And of His kingdom there will be no end."
34 Then Mary said to the angel, "How can this be, since I do not know a man?"
35 The angel answered her, "The Holy Spirit will come upon you, and the power of the Highest will overshadow you. Therefore the Holy One who will be born will be called the Son of God. 36 Listen, your cousin Elizabeth has also conceived a son in her old age. And this is the sixth month with her who was declared barren. 37 For with God nothing will be impossible."
38 Mary said, "I am the servant of the Lord. May it be unto me according to your word." Then the angel departed from her.

Throughout Mary's life, she hid the word of God in her heart. If she didn't understand something, she kept it believing that one day God would make it clear. Although I am sure there would have been negative words spoken about an engaged girl being pregnant before marriage, she didn't complain about it. She didn't even try to defend herself against Joseph's decision to put her away quietly. That means he would have found a place for her to live but didn't believe her story and didn't want to marry her. God himself spoke to Joseph in a dream through an angel. After his encounter with God, Joseph marries Mary and obeys God.

Pray about its meaning

Mary didn't understand the prophecies about her child, but she kept those things believing they were important.

Luke 2: 19 But Mary kept all these things and pondered them in her heart.

Daniel sought God for understanding

Daniel was a captive in Babylon. He lived his life as a slave but was given much privilege and promotion by the kings he served as wise man. Daniel was given interpretation of dreams. Daniel was given words of wisdom. God was using Daniel as a prophet in Babylon (an enemy of Israel).

God gave Daniel a special dream that scared him because he knew it was a dream from God, but he had not been given the revelation of its meaning. What he did is seek God for 3 weeks in pray and fasting continuously about the interpretation of the dream. It is exactly what a person should do if God gives you a dream or speaks to you and you don`t know its meaning: seek God.

Daniel 9: 2 in the first year of his reign, I, Daniel, observed in the books the number of the years which were specified by the word of the Lord to Jeremiah the prophet for the accomplishment of the desolations of Jerusalem, that is, seventy years. 3 I set my face toward the Lord God to seek by prayer and supplications with fasting and sackcloth and ashes.

Because of his constant prayer, finally after the 3rd week, an angel was sent to speak to Daniel and give him the interpretation of the dream. The angel explained that the moment Daniel began to fast and pray, God sent the angel to bring the answer but there were demons who tried to stop him from getting Daniel the answer to prayer. This information is important to all people who pray, if for no other reason than to know that persistence in prayer is important because there are spiritual authorities and powers that we cannot see. Also, that God immediately answers prayer. The angel revealed the future to Daniel. The prophetic dreams were written as a parallel to the book of Revelation in talking about things that have not yet happened: of kingdoms, rulers and the end of the age.

Through Daniels's praying to understand the dream, we God's people are given a glimpse into the future. We are given information about Israel but also the antichrist and ruling nations.

It is not technique

Not the tone or the words alone – not simply a certain scripture for everyone - individualized prayer depending on person, the moment, the season. God instructs us to communicate with him in private. It is different than congregational prayer. God instructs us to speak to God plainly and not just repeat words thinking that the quantity of prayer makes it more valuable. In some other religions, people say the exact same words over and over believing that it gives the prayers power because of the repetition.

Matthew 6: 6 But you, when you pray, enter your closet, and when you have shut your door, pray to your Father who is in secret. And your Father who sees in secret will reward you openly. 7 But when you pray, do not use vain repetitions, as the heathen do.

It is not in learned prayers alone

Jesus taught his disciples how to pray. It is a prayer prayed around the world; it is known as the LORD's prayer. It covers all aspects of human life including basic needs as well as spiritual strength and giving worship to God. Although it is an excellent prayer, it is not the only prayer.

Matthew 6: 9 "Therefore pray in this manner:
Our Father who is in heaven,
hallowed be Your name.
10 Your kingdom come;
Your will be done
   on earth, as it is in heaven.
11 Give us this day our daily bread.
12 And forgive us our debts,
   as we forgive our debtors.
13 And lead us not into temptation,
   but deliver us from evil.
For Yours is the kingdom and the power and the glory forever. Amen.

There are many other prayers mentioned in the Bible that can be prayed. In 1549 the Anglican book of prayer was released. It is a book filled with prayers for all types of occasions. There is a catholic book of prayer as well. Many denominations have books of prayers that people have been inspirited to write. Although these prayers are not equal to scripture by any means, I don`t deny they could be used to help people to pray. I am certainly not against using any type of prayer that helps people to communicate with God. There are prayers that are written. It is one way of praying – reading prayers with faith. It is not the only way to pray and most of the saints in the scriptures did not have a written prayer or scripture to pray.

Most prayer is conversation with God such as you would speak with a most intimate friend. If you cannot communicate with God without this personal, intimate giving of yourself to God, you are not truly entering into the glory of being an intercessor. The type of prayer I am speaking of is intimate, personal, connecting, fellowship – speaking with God as with your closest friend.

The Apostles and prophets wrote our scripture inspired by God. They instruct us in some types of prayer. The Apostle Paul in the Book of Ephesians specifically leads us in ways to pray for spiritual growth.

Ephesians 1: 17 so that the God of our Lord Jesus Christ, the Father of glory, may give you the Spirit of wisdom and revelation in the knowledge of Him, 18 that the eyes of your understanding may be enlightened, that you may know what is the hope of His calling and what are the riches of the glory of His inheritance among the saints, 19 and what is the surpassing greatness of His power toward us who believe, according to the working of His mighty power, 20 which He performed in Christ when He raised Him from the dead and seated Him at His own right hand in the heavenly places, 21 far above all principalities, and power, and might, and dominion, and every name that is named, not only in this age but also in that which is to come.

The Apostle Paul not only gives us some excellent prayers in the book of Ephesians but in all of his writings there are some prayers and prayer insights. The Apostle lets us know that it is not just in his words alone. It is not in his strength alone but the Holy Spirit living in him and through him that he ministered to the people.

1 Corinthians 2: 2 Brothers, when I came to you, I did not come with

superiority of speech or wisdom, declaring to you the testimony of God. 2 For I determined not to know anything among you except Jesus Christ and Him crucified. 3 I was with you in weakness and in fear and in much trembling. 4 My speech and my preaching was not with enticing words of man's wisdom, but in demonstration of the Spirit and of power, 5 so that your faith should not stand in the wisdom of men, but in the power of God.

Consistent prayer

It is normal for a spirit- filled Christian that each day should be a day in prayer and with a readiness to pray Living in the presence of God and communicating with God regularly is a special privilege we have as Christians. Not all people know how special it is. Not all people use their privileges. It is possible to live in constant communion with God because God the Holy Spirit lives on the inside of us. We don't have to break through the heavens to pray. We already have Christ living on the inside of us in the person of the Holy Spirit. We can commune with God because we are constantly in His presence. The apostle Paul knew this type of communion with God and encouraged us to pray without ceasing.

Galatians 5: 25 If we live in the Spirit, let us also walk in the Spirit.

1 Thessalonians 5: 16 Rejoice always. 17 Pray without ceasing. 18 In everything give thanks, for this is the will of God in Christ Jesus concerning you.

If prayer were only religious, in a certain place, during a church service or even congregational prayer, it would be impossible to pray without ceasing. The Apostle Paul is letting us know God is omnipresent. He is with each of us always in the person of the Holy Spirit. Quick prayers as you pass someone on the street or in a store are just as important as longer ones. It is the willingness to intercede for others that is the important part.

There will be aspects of the supernatural because Jehovah God really is God. Jesus Christ is our Saviour and the Holy Spirit dwells within believers.

Please do not think I believe it is a light thing that God should dwell within me. I know it is impossible for me to ever obtain worth. It is impossible that omnipotent God, creator of all things, completely Holy hating sin, could dwell in me in my own righteousness. But it is the righteousness of God in Christ that makes me Holy. Jesus Christ's blood applied to my life makes me Holy. It is Jesus Holiness imparted unto me that makes it possible for the Holy Spirit to live in me and through me.

2 Corinthians 5: 21 God made Him who knew no sin to be sin for us, that we might become the righteousness of God in Him.

The people of Israel feared God because He is Holy, and they were sinners. There was no atonement yet made for sin, so the appearance of God was mighty and scary to the people. Moses talked directly to God and was as a mediator or intercessor for Israel. Afterwards Aaron and the Levites were the intercessors and priests of Israel.

Exodus 19: 16 So on the third day, in the morning, there was thunder and lightning, and a thick cloud on the mountain, and the sound of an exceedingly loud trumpet. All the people who were in the camp trembled. 17 Then Moses brought the people out of the camp to meet with God, and they stood at the foot of the mountain. 18 Now Mount Sinai was completely covered in smoke because the Lord had descended upon it in fire, and the smoke ascended like the smoke of a furnace, and the whole mountain shook violently. 19 When the sound of the trumpet grew louder and louder, Moses spoke, and God answered him with a voice.[a]

Jesus Christ's shed blood for us means entrance into the Holy of Holies. Jesus is the only intercessor or high priest that we need. He lives to make intercession for us. Because we live in Christ, because Christ lives in us, we have constant communication.

Hebrews 10: 19 Therefore, brothers, we have confidence to enter the Most Holy Place by the blood of Jesus, 20 by a new and living way that He has opened for us through the veil, that is to say, His flesh, 21 and since we have a High Priest over the house of God, 22 let us draw near with a true heart in full assurance of faith, having our hearts sprinkled to cleanse them from an evil conscience, and our bodies washed with pure water. 23 Let us firmly hold the profession of our faith without wavering, for He who promised is faithful.

It is transformational

Being in the presence of God transforms a person. Each encounter with God in prayer, praise, worship or Bible reading, causes us to be more Christlike. God is light. We are transformed by His light. We become more like him as we are in His presence. The truth of it was first shown in the character of Moses who approached God to intercede for Israel. The radiance of God's glory shone on Moses so that he placed a veil over his face because the people were scared of the light that shone on him.

Exodus 34: 29 When Moses came down from Mount Sinai with the two tablets of testimony in the hands of Moses, when he came down from the mountain, Moses did not know that the skin of his face shone while he talked with Him. 30 So when Aaron and all the children of Israel saw Moses, amazingly, the skin of his face shone, and they were afraid to come near him. 31 But Moses called to them, and Aaron and all the rulers of the congregation returned to him, and Moses spoke to them. 32 Afterward all the children of Israel drew near, and he commanded them all that the Lord had spoken to him on Mount Sinai.

33 When Moses finished speaking with them, he put a veil over his face. 34 But whenever Moses went in before the Lord to speak with Him, he took the veil off until he came out. Then he came out and spoke to the children of Israel what he had been commanded. 35 The children of Israel saw the face of Moses, that the skin of Moses' face shone, and then Moses put the veil over his face again until he went in to speak with Him.

2 Corinthians 3: 18 But we all, seeing the glory of the Lord with unveiled faces, as in a mirror, are being transformed into the same image from glory to glory by the Spirit of the Lord

Life beyond all earthly joy

Living in the presence of God constantly is a joy and pleasure beyond all human comprehension or comparison. It is closer than a marriage because we live in God and His Spirit lives in us. A non-Christian cannot understand it. A Christian should know it but unfortunately not all do. Some Christians do not live in the rights given to them by God. As Christians, we can always pray. As Christians, we can read God's word and know His will and do it. These are parts of the privilege. The joy of living with God is more awesome than anything a person can imagine.

Ephesians 1: 17 so that the God of our Lord Jesus Christ, the Father of glory, may give you the Spirit of wisdom and revelation in the knowledge of Him, 18 that the eyes of your understanding may be enlightened, that you may know what is the hope of His calling and what are the riches of the glory of His inheritance among the saints, 19 and what is the surpassing greatness of His power toward us who believe, according to the working of His mighty power, 20 which He performed in Christ when He raised Him from the dead and seated Him at His own right hand in the heavenly places,

21 far above all principalities, and power, and might, and dominion, and every name that is named, not only in this age but also in that which is to come.

Radical Fundamentalism

Living in the Spirit means pursuing God wholly each day of your life. It means God is the priority. Please realize that it differs for all people, not all people can go up on a mountain to pray for 40 days like Moses. Not all people pray 2 or more hours a day. The most important thing for you decide as reading this book is the depth of relationship you desire with God. Only you choose the level of intimacy with God. He is always willing to be in communion with us.

There are radical fundamentalists in many world religions. Radical fundamentalist has a nasty connotation to it. I do want to acknowledge Roberts Liardon for teaching me that being called a radical fundamentalist is not bad. Radical is choosing God first always for all your life long. Radical is believing every word of the Bible and living with it as a guide for all decisions in life. Most people would understand it in the concept if I were speaking of nuns or priests. For some reason people don't understand it concerning charismatics or Pentecostals. The truth is that we are priests of the New Covenant of Jesus according to the scriptures.

1 Peter 2: 9 But you are a chosen race, a royal priesthood, a holy nation, a people for God's own possession, so that you may declare the goodness of Him who has called you out of darkness into His marvelous light. 10 In times past, you were not a people, but now you are the people of God. You had not received mercy, but now you have received mercy.

Radical

If you want to be average, you fit God into your life. There is a place for God, a place for sports, a place for things and people. That is a secular humanist view of religion. It is not a Christian perspective. None of the disciples of Jesus who were martyred for their faith, lived ordinary, average lives. Their lives had been so radically changed by Jesus Christ that they could not help but speak the things they spoke or do the things they did.

The essential thing I am speaking of is desire towards God. It is the very reason you became a Christian. It is the reason you live as a Christian. Fundamentalism is literally believing the scriptures to be true and without error. Yes. There are radical fundamentalists in other religions who will kill innocent people because of their faith. The difference between those religions and Christianity is that Christians who are radical and fundamentalist would die for Christ. Never would they kill because of God.

Presently, there are nations in the earth where Christians are persecuted and martyred for their faith. They are going about their private lives not against any people. They do not bomb people. They do not kill people. They simply worship their God, share the truths of God with others with love and serving and giving. The people who hate Christians and kill them are radical and fundamental alright – but it is ungodly - demonic.

Jehovah God in the person of the LORD Jesus Christ taught us to love, to serve, to give, to express love by praying for people, serving them, healing them, teaching them. Our God loves people. Hatred is a sin and it should be repented of. Prejudice or ethnic hatred of people is a sin and it is not inspired by God. Clearly Jesus came to bring the truth of God's love for people by sacrificing His life so that we may all be saved should we believe in Him. Being a Christian means radically living your life by God's Word, loving God with all your being and loving people. Characteristics of a radical Christian, include, love, mercy, kindness, gentleness, meekness, humility and serving others.

No one can determine your desire towards God besides you. If you want Him with all your being, He will manifest His presence towards you.

Jeremiah 29: 11 For I know the plans that I have for you, says the Lord, plans for peace and not for evil, to give you a future and a hope. 12 Then you shall call upon Me, and you shall come and pray to Me, and I will listen to you. 13 You shall seek Me and find Me, when you shall search for Me with all your heart.

Deuteronomy 4: 29 But if from there you will seek the Lord your God, you will find Him, if you seek Him with all your heart and with all your soul.

Ways that God speaks to people

Dreams, visions, scriptures, phrases, other people, preaching or teaching, your own words, through unusual means such as symbols in nature or through situations.

Speaking to God is not one way only. It is a conversation. God can speak one word and radically transform your life.

1 Thessalonians 5: 15 See that no one renders evil for evil to anyone. But always seek to do good to one another and to all.

16 Rejoice always. 17 Pray without ceasing. 18 In everything give thanks, for this is the will of God in Christ Jesus concerning you.
Dreams

God can give a person a dream that is different and the person will know it is a dream from God. The person's spirit will be communing with God while the person is sleeping. God communicates the truths to the person by images, scenes, video and audio. God gives the dream. It is a normal way for God to communicate with His people especially if they are not aware of the situation God wants to show them.

Joseph had several notable dreams given to him as a youth. He knew that the dream was from God but didn't know how to interpret it and told his family about it in a way that made him seem he was bragging. They despised him for it.

Genesis 37: 9 9 Then he dreamed another dream and told it to his brothers and said, "I have dreamed another dream. The sun and the moon and eleven stars were bowing to me."

Joseph should have prayed asking God for the meaning of the dream. It is excellent that you know God has spoken to you in a dream. That is the starting point, not the conclusion. The next things the person should do is pray. Literally ask God to reveal the meaning of the dream to you. Don't trust your own self to interpret what God has given you. That would be an error.

1. Recognize the dream is from God. Thank Him for the dream.
2. Pray – seek God specifically about the meaning to the dream. Later in life, as the truth of Joseph's dream from God came to pass and the very thing God had shown him in a dream from his youth, Joseph uses wisdom that only comes from knowing God. While imprisoned in Pharaoh's jail for a crime he did not commit, Joseph is told dreams by both the Baker and the winetaster who were thrown into jail because someone had stolen something from Pharaoh.

Joseph knows they both had unusual dreams believing that God would give the interpretation of them. He did not presume to interpret them himself. Please see Joseph has gained wisdom and faith in God.

The High Life

Genesis 40: 8 Then Joseph said to them, "Do not interpretations belong to God? Please tell them to me."

9 The chief cupbearer told his dream to Joseph and said to him, "In my dream, a vine was in front of me. 10 And in the vine there were three branches. As it budded, its blossoms shot forth and its clusters brought forth ripe grapes. 11 Pharaoh's cup was in my hand, and I took the grapes, and pressed them into Pharaoh's cup, and I put the cup into Pharaoh's hand."

12 Joseph said to him, "This is the interpretation of it. The three branches are three days. 13 Within three days Pharaoh will lift up your head and restore you to your place, and you will deliver Pharaoh's cup into his hand in the same way you did before when you were his cupbearer. 14 But remember me when it is well with you, and show kindness, I pray you, to me, and make mention of me to Pharaoh, and get me out of this house. 15 For I was indeed kidnapped out of the land of the Hebrews, and I have done nothing that they should put me in the dungeon."

16 When the chief baker saw that the interpretation was good, he said to Joseph, "I also was in my dream, and I had three white baskets on my head. 17 In the uppermost basket there was all manner of baked goods for Pharaoh, and the birds ate them out of the basket on my head."

18 Joseph answered and said, "This is the interpretation: The three baskets are three days. 19 Within three days Pharaoh will lift your head from off you and will hang you on a tree, and the birds will eat your flesh from you."

20 It happened on the third day, which was Pharaoh's birthday, that he made a feast for all his servants. He lifted up the heads of the chief cupbearer and the chief baker among his servants. 21 He restored the chief cupbearer to his position again, and he put the cup into Pharaoh's hand. 22 However, he hanged the chief baker, just as Joseph had interpreted to them.

  Joseph correctly interprets the dreams, because God gives him the interpretation. Not all people who get dreams from God immediately get the interpretation. Kings would often have wise men to interpret dreams and symbols and things for him. Usually, they were like wizards or magicians. In the scriptures both Daniel and Joseph were used to interpret dreams for kings. Two years later after the wine taster was released from prison as Joseph interpreted, he remembered Joseph's interpretation of his dream. He remembers him because Pharaoh has a dream but does not know the interpretation (Genesis 41). Joseph is presented to Pharaoh. Joseph does not trust his own interpretation of the dream. He says God is the one who will give the interpretation.

Genesis 41: 16 Joseph answered Pharaoh, saying, "It is not in me. God will give Pharaoh a favorable answer."

God does give Joseph the interpretation of the dream. Because Joseph gets the interpretation, Pharaoh makes him a ruler second in command. Joseph does not only have the wisdom to communicate with God concerning dreams, Joseph uses wisdom from God to help rule the nation of Egypt while there were years of plenty and while there were years of famine.

It is essential, after God gives you the interpretation not to speak foolishly but to state exactly what God has told you to the correct people. It may be to no one. God used Joseph to help Egypt and Israel during those years. Joseph did not speak to just anyone. He spoke directly to the person who was the authority decision maker. He had learned not to talk spiritual things to just anyone. He realized God doesn't speak for no reason. God speaks to communicate. After the interpretation, Joseph gives God all the glory and does not boast that God has used him to interpret.

Should we get a dream from God, we should pray for the interpretation. Should someone speak to us a dream, we should pray for wisdom that God may give the interpretation.

Humility

Important with all aspects of God communicating with you is humility, wisdom and discernment. These are character traits that are not necessarily present in the person God uses until the person has learned from God. Character is developed rather than imparted or gifted. Godly character is only developed by being in God's presence, honouring God's Word and worshipping only God. Through communion with God, a believer can develop godly traits or fruit of the Spirit. There is no way a person can willfully gain these traits if he or she does not have them. They are only developed by communion with the Creator.

Visions

Visions are similar to dreams because God communicates to a person an idea or shows the person something. Just as a dreamer knows that God has spoken to him in a dream, so will the person know God has spoken to him in a vision. The difference is the person who has the vision is going about his business in the day and God shows up. It is never for no reason. God does not communicate for entertainment or for jest or for no reason. God only communicates if it is important.

An example of a vision is when Elisha got a vision of his servant Gehazi being unfaithful. Elisha had said to Naaman who was healed of leprosy that no gifts would be received. Gehazi, sees potential to exploit Naaman without anyone knowing. He rides to meet with Nehman and lies saying his master wanted some robes and money. His perversion of twisting a miracle of healing into a money-making scheme fails when Elisha is shown the situation by God through a word of knowledge. Elisha reports on what Gehazi had done and curses him because he tried to exploit the healing power of God.

2 Kings 5: 26 He said to him, "Did my heart not go with you when the man turned from his chariot to meet you? Is it a time to take money, and to take garments, olives and vineyards, sheep and oxen, male and female servants? 27 The leprosy of Naaman will cling to you and to your descendants forever." So he went out from his presence, leprous like snow.

Never prostitute God's gifts

It is essential should God show you a vision that you pray for an interpretation. It is important that you never defile yourself by trying to use God's presence, miracles, healings or other aspects of God for money. Balam was a prophet of God but he had a nasty character in that he wanted money and fame more than obeying God. The King Balak knew that Balaam was a prophet. The signs of a prophet were on his life because he could pronounce blessings on someone. The king sends for him.

Numbers 22: 5"A people went out from Egypt. They cover the face of the earth, and they dwell next to me. 6 And now, please come curse this people for me because they are too mighty for me. Perhaps I will prevail, and we will defeat them, and I will drive them out of the land because I know that he whom you bless is blessed, and he whom you curse is cursed."

Balaam seems to be a righteous prophet because he does not answer the kings' men without praying about the matter. God speaks to Balaam clearly.

Numbers 22: 12 God said to Balaam, "You will not go with them. You will not curse the people because they are blessed."

We see the lust for wealth in Balaam that when the kings' men return with a wealthy offer for him he goes to God again about the same matter even though God spoke His will already.

Numbers 22: 15 Again Balak sent officials, more numerous and more honorable than they. 16 They came to Balaam and said to him,

"Thus says Balak the son of Zippor, 'Please, let nothing hold you back from coming to me, 17 because I will promote you to very great honor, and anything you say to me I will do. Come please, curse this people for me.'"

18 Balaam answered the servants of Balak, "If Balak gave me his house full of silver and gold, I am not able to go beyond the command of the Lord my God, to do less or more. 19 Now please remain here tonight, that I may know what more the Lord will say to me."

The sin of Balaam

Balaam's second request to God was not based on information. He knew it was God's will to bless Israel. His response to the men was based on his greed at an offer of wealth. Truly in the story of Balaam, God shows how he used even Balaam to bless Israel. The importance I am emphasizing through is that person receiving communications from God remain humble and not given to covetousness. Praying for discernment and for God to keep your heart pure as well as having wisdom are all characteristics necessary for any servant of God or prophet of God.

Temptations for those who serve God are usually 1) pride 2) sexual impurity 3) wealth and fame.

1 John 1: 16 For all that is in the world—the lust of the flesh, the lust of the eyes, and the pride of life—is not of the Father but is of the world. 17 The world and its desires are passing away, but the one who does the will of God lives forever.

Because the person is communicating with God, much favour will be shown to the person. God will place a shield of favour around the person (Psalm 5:12). A person who communicates with God is desirable because one word from God can change a nation or a people or a destiny. The only way to overcome the temptations that will surely come are to recognize you are being tempted, pray, avoid situations where you could give into them.

Jesus literally taught us to pray that we not enter in to temptation.

With God's help, a person can live in integrity, especially since we now have the Holy Spirit living on the inside of us. The truth is godly character must be so strong in you that your spirit is stronger than your soul or will. You can live by the Word of God if you are living in the Spirit.
Praying regularly and reading and confessing scriptures are ways to strengthen your inner man. They directly build up your spirit.

Scripture

The RHEMA Word of God. God, or God inspired Word, can illuminate the scriptures to you as you are reading scripture. What occurs is that the Holy Spirit living on the inside of you reveals the scriptures, so they jump out at you. It's like a spiritual highlighter. The words jump out of the pages at you. You immediately know the scriptures are special for you. The meaning of the words becomes clear and without a doubt, you know God is speaking to you. What is necessary is that you keep a habit of prayer and scripture reading regularly.

It is usual that during these periods of quiet study and worship that God may reveal the meaning of the scriptures to you. It is one of the awesome things about serving God, the Scriptures are God's Word, His expressed will towards us. The Holy Spirit inspired believing men to write them. The author of the scriptures lives in you and can interpret the scriptures as you read them so that they apply to your life and give you light or revelation. Wisdom comes from reading God's word. Because it gives us important information on how to pray, as well as teaches us God's will, as well as special insight or revelation for a situation of our lives, it is essential that we read the Bible regularly.

Joshua 1: 7 Be strong and very courageous, in order to act carefully in accordance with all the law that My servant Moses commanded you. Do not turn aside from it to the right or the left, so that you may succeed wherever you go. 8 This Book of the Law must not depart from your mouth. Meditate on it day and night so that you may act carefully according to all that is written in it. For then you will make your way successful, and you will be wise. 9 Have not I commanded you? Be strong and courageous. Do not be afraid or dismayed, for the Lord your God is with you wherever you go."

Even as Joshua was commanded to keep the Word of God in his mouth, to meditate on it and to obey it, we should be constantly feeding the spirit man with scripture. As we read the word, pray the word, meditate on the word, confess the word and talk about the word, it becomes engrafted into our very souls. It becomes a part of us. We become as living epistles. It means, we believe it, live by it and make all decisions because of it. The Word of God is the foundation of our lives and also the plumb line. The only foundation that will endure is one built on God's Word. Jesus Christ is the corner stone. The truths of the scriptures are our only firm foundation. It is a plumb line because as we align our lives to God's Word, we are truly making decisions based on scripture. It means we are living a life pleasing to God.

Revealed Wisdom

Just as a believer knows if God has spoken to him through any means, so for certain will the scriptures jump out at you as words from God. You will in that moment know that God is directly speaking to you and you will get wisdom on how to apply the scripture in your life. There are such gifted people throughout the scriptures, but I will mention only some who were given special wisdom or knowledge.

Men of Issachar

They were given wisdom and knowledge of the times and seasons. Discerning the season you are in is essential to functioning in the spirit. It would be foolish to try to plant in winter. The place I live is cold and there is snow. Planting should be done in the spring or the fall. It is essential to discern the conditions you are living in from a spiritual point of view. The best way to do this is to pray for discernment specifically.

1 Chronicles 12: 32 From the sons of Issachar, those having understanding of times and what Israel should do: two hundred of their captains with all their brothers at their command.

Bereans

They did not trust in preaching without the scriptures themselves. They searched the scriptures to see if were true. These people believed the written scriptures more than the Apostles' preaching. As they searched the scripture and found it to be true, they valued the preachers. It is an excellent model for us to follow. The scripture must be viewed as being the highest authority in all things concerning human life.

Acts 17: 10 The brothers immediately sent Paul and Silas away by night to

Berea. When they arrived, they went into the synagogue of the Jews. 11 These were more noble than those in Thessalonica, for they received the word with all eagerness, daily examining the Scriptures, to find out if these things were so. 12 Therefore many of them believed, including honorable Greek women and many Greek men.

Apostle Peter

God gives a word of knowledge to the Apostle Peter quickening the Rhema Word of God to him in Acts 2 after the outpouring of the Holy Spirit on the day of Pentecost. All of the 120 disciples of Jesus prayed and experienced the baptism of the Holy Spirit in the upper room. They were compelled into the streets below with pilgrims of all the nations gathered there to celebrate the feast of Pentecost. Peter gets a special word of knowledge that they are experiencing the outpouring of the Holy Spirit as described by the prophet Joel. It is a way of discerning the spiritual seasons in the light of God's word.

Acts 2: 16 But this is what was spoken by the prophet Joel:

17 'In the last days it shall be,' says God,
    'that I will pour out My Spirit on all flesh;
your sons and your daughters shall prophesy,
    your young men shall see visions,
    and your old men shall dream dreams.

The Rhema Word is God's Word. What it means is that God gives you revelation or insight on how to apply it to your life. The Word of God is living. It is multidimensional. It is complex. It proves itself by confirming itself even though there are 66 books written over thousands of years. God can give revelation to you one day and show you a different revelation or a different dimension of it a different day. Because the Word is God inspired and the Holy Spirit resides within you, you can keep getting revelation and knowledge throughout your life from the scriptures.

Preaching and teaching of the Scripture

Pastors and ministers that speak in church prayerfully consider what to teach the people. The Holy Spirit inspires them to create sermons that will teach, build up and nourish the congregation.

1 Corinthians 2: 4 My speech and my preaching was not with enticing words of man's wisdom, but in demonstration of the Spirit and of power, 5 so that your faith should not stand in the wisdom of men, but in the power

of God.

The most usual way that most Christians hear from God is through their pastors in church services. God inspires the pastors with a message and scriptures. Often a Christian in the right church will hear from God through his or her pastor's messages. It will seem that the words the minister is preaching are directly speaking to him or her personally. Either a word or phrase or scripture will be exactly the word that will apply to the person's life. It will most often confirm something you are praying about.

Other means

The truth is God can speak to you in any way that you will receive from Him. God used Balaam's donkey to speak to him. Because Balaam was given to covetousness, he went to Balak to try to curse Israel. On the way, an angel of the LORD blocked the way. The donkey saw the angel and stopped and would not continue. Balaam in anger, beat his donkey. Finally, God caused the donkey to speak. If it had not been for that donkey stopping, the angel of the LORD would have slain Balaam for his disobedience to God. God can use anyone He chooses to speak to us.

Numbers 22: 28 Then the Lord opened the mouth of the donkey, and she said to Balaam, "What have I done to you, that you have struck me these three times?"

29 And Balaam said to the donkey, "You have mocked me. O that there was a sword in my hand, for now I would kill you."

30 The donkey said to Balaam, "Am I not your donkey, whom you have ridden since I became yours, to this day? Do I normally do this to you?" And he said, "No."

Situations

God may speak to you in your life by the situation you are in. God can use anything to teach us if our spirits are teachable. We should pray and expect God to teach us. The Holy Spirit can give us information and insight into all aspects of our human lives including our jobs. There are prophets who have had God speak to them through their circumstances and used their circumstances to speak to all of Israel. Most of the prophets' lives were this way. God can use any situation in our lives to reveal truths to us.

The High Life

Isaiah

Isaiah was called by God to speak his word in a unique way. First, he had seen the goodness of the king, Uzziah, who was mostly an excellent king for Israel. It was only later in Uzziah's life that pride and disobedience to God was manifest. Uzziah, a king with wealth, fame, and peace desired to offer incense to God. It was only allowed by Levites. The King was not a priest. The king disobeyed God's commandments that only the priest may enter the temple and do this sacrifice. The high priest warned him and commanded him to stop. The king, who had been good for Israel for many years, was overcome in his lust to disobey God. Because of his sin, he died a leper.

2 Chronicles 26: 16 And as he grew strong, his heart grew more proud, leading to his destruction. Then he acted unfaithfully against the Lord his God, for he entered the temple main hall of the Lord to burn incense on the altar. 17 But Azariah the priest entered in after him, and with him were eighty priests of the Lord—men of valor. 18 And they stood against King Uzziah and said to him, "It is not for you, Uzziah, to burn incense to the Lord for it is for the priests, the sons of Aaron, who are consecrated to burn incense. Leave from the sanctuary because you have been unfaithful, and there will be no honor for you from the Lord God."

19 Then Uzziah was enraged, and in his hand was a censer for incense. And when he became angry with the priests, leprosy appeared on his forehead in front of the priests in the house of the Lord, near the altar of incense. 20 Then Azariah the head priest and all the priests turned to him, and he had leprosy on his forehead; and they hastened to remove him from there, and he also hurried to leave because the Lord had struck him.

Isaiah had served the king. Truly he knew that a righteous king had become sinful and died in his sin. Because of it, there were many changes in Israel. It would have ripped out his heart to know that a righteous God appointed leader had died. Yet, even though this horrible event occurred, Isaiah also had a direct visitation from God. The glory of God was so strong that it overwhelmed him. He saw the glory of God and the angels guarding him. He was immediately aware of the holiness of God and his own unrighteousness as well as the peoples. He confessed it.

Isaiah 6: 1 In the year that King Uzziah died I saw the Lord sitting on a throne, high and lifted up, and His train filled the temple. 2 Above it stood the seraphim. Each one had six wings. With two he covered his face, and with two he covered his feet, and with two he flew. 3 One cried to another and said:

"Holy, holy, holy, is the Lord of Hosts;
   the whole earth is full of His glory."

4 The posts of the door moved at the voice of him who cried, and the house was filled with smoke.

5 And I said: "Woe is me! For I am undone because I am a man of unclean lips, and I dwell in the midst of a people of unclean lips. For my eyes have seen the King, the Lord of Hosts."

Because Isaiah's response to God's Holy presence is sincere and humble, God releases one of the angels to purge his lips with a coal from the altar of God. His mouth is sanctified by it. He is cleansed and set apart to speak for God.

Isaiah 6: 6 Then one of the seraphim flew to me with a live coal which he had taken with the tongs from off the altar in his hand. 7 And he laid it on my mouth, and said, "This has touched your lips, and your iniquity is taken away, and your sin purged."

The next part of his calling is Isaiah's acceptance of the LORD's calling. He willfully accepts the commission to speak for God.

Isaiah 6: 8 Also I heard the voice of the Lord saying, "Whom shall I send, and who will go for us?"

Then I said, "Here am I. Send me."

Isaiah is used to speak to Israel and also to kings. He speaks judgement; He also prophesies of the coming of the Messiah. In Isaiah 8, he names his son after the word of God that God is speaking to him. All of his life was as a message to Israel. God gave him special warning not to make agreement with the unrighteous people.

Isaiah 8: 11 For the Lord spoke thus to me with a strong hand and instructed me that I should not walk in the way of this people, saying:
   12 You should not say, "It is a conspiracy,"
      concerning all that this people calls a conspiracy,
neither fear their threats
   nor be afraid of them.

The High Life

Many of God's prophets had to be protected from the people of Israel and from the kings and rulers of Israel. The prophets heard from God. Not all people liked what God was speaking to them. Isaiah was specifically chosen by God to be used throughout his life to witness to Israel to repent and return to God.

Jeremiah

The prophet Jeremiah was chosen by God to be a prophet of Israel. First, even though Jeremiah knew God was speaking to him, he doubted that he could do what God was telling him. Jeremiah truly did not know the might of his God. The consecration of Jeremiah is certain. It comes directly from God.

Jeremiah 1: 4 Now the word of the Lord came to me, saying,

5 "Before I formed you in the womb I knew you;
and before you were born I sanctified you,
and I ordained you a prophet to the nations."

6 Then I said, "Ah, Lord God! Truly, I cannot speak, for I am a youth."

7 But the Lord said to me, "Do not say, 'I am a youth.' For you shall go everywhere that I send you, and whatever I command you, you shall speak. 8 Do not be afraid of their faces. For I am with you to deliver you," says the Lord.

9 Then the Lord put forth His hand and touched my mouth. And the Lord said to me, "Now, I have put My words in your mouth. 10 See, I have this day set you over the nations and over the kingdoms, to root out and to pull down, to destroy and to throw down, to build and to plant."

Jeremiah was chosen to speak to Israel as well as the king of Israel who was living in sin and serving idols. The king did not listen to Jeremiah but imprisoned him for his prophecies because God used Jeremiah to warn Israel to repent or the Babylonians would come, fight against them and overtake them. His words may have sounded like treason because he was speaking harsh judgements of God. Many people did not believe him. The king finally believes him towards the end of his reign before Babylon invades them, but he cares what the people think of him more than he values the Word of God. Jeremiah had spoken that if they would surrender, their lives would be spared.

During the years of his ministry as prophet speaking to the people and the king, he was thrown into prison, beaten and abused, thrown into a muddy pit, He endured much abuse in his own country. The truth though is he was an example to the nation of Israel of what would happen to them if they did not repent.

Jeremiah 38: 6 Then they took Jeremiah and cast him into the cistern of Malkijah the son of Hammelech that was in the court of the prison, and they let Jeremiah down with cords. And in the cistern there was no water, only mud, so Jeremiah sank in the mud.

Ironically, after enduring much suffering because he spoke the truth of God to Israel and the king, Jeremiah is set free and given a financial reward by the invading king of Babylon who conquers Israel. Jeremiah was respected by officials of the nation who conquered them.

Jeremiah 40: 2 The captain of the guard had taken Jeremiah and said to him: "The Lord your God has pronounced this disaster upon this place. 3 And the Lord has brought it and done according as He has said. Because you have sinned against the Lord, and have not obeyed His voice, therefore this thing has come upon you. 4 Now look, I am loosening you this day from the chains which are on your hands. If it seems good to you to come with me to Babylon, come and I will look well after you. But if it seems bad to you to come with me into Babylon, never mind. See, all the land is before you. Go wherever it seems good and right for you to go." 5 Now while he was not yet going back, he said, "Go back also to Gedaliah the son of Ahikam, the son of Shaphan, whom the king of Babylon has made governor over the cities of Judah, and dwell with him among the people. Or go wherever it seems right for you to go."

So the captain of the guard gave him rations and a gift and let him go. 6 Then Jeremiah went to Gedaliah the son of Ahikam to Mizpah and lived with him among the people who were left in the land.

God often has used the situations of lives of the prophets to speak to Israel: Jeremiah, Ezekiel, Hosea

Ezekiel

The calling of Ezekiel is also supernatural because Ezekiel sees heavenly visions of creatures (angels) who appear to him so that he falls to the ground at their magnificence. It is after this encounter with the supernatural that immediately God speaks to him and calls him to be a prophet of Israel. Ezekiel is chosen to speak warning to sinners and is told that if they repent, they will be spared but if they don't repent and he has warned them, he will be innocent. He is also warned that if he fails to warn them at God's command, their blood will be upon him.

Ezekiel 2: 1 Then He said to me: Son of man, stand on your feet, and I will speak to you! 2 When He spoke to me, the Spirit entered me and set me on my feet. Then I heard Him speaking to me.

3 And He said to me: Son of man, I send you to the sons of Israel, to a rebellious nation that has rebelled against Me. They and their fathers have transgressed against Me even to this very day. 4 And as for the impudent and obstinate children, I am sending you to them. And you shall say to them, "Thus says the Lord God." 5 As for them, whether they listen or not (for they are a rebellious house), they shall know that there has been a prophet among them. 6 And you, son of man, do not be afraid of them or be afraid of their words, though briers and thorns be with you, and you dwell among scorpions. Do not be afraid of their words or be dismayed at their looks, for they are a rebellious house. 7 You shall speak My words to them, whether they listen or not, for they are rebellious. 8 But you, son of man, hear what I say to you. Do not be rebellious like that rebellious house. Open your mouth and eat what I give you.

As a prophet, he is responsible to say exactly as God tells him. There is an eternal weight to his words. He is warned that although he will speak what God says, people will not obey. He also is given prophecy about the siege of Jerusalem. He not only speaks it, he demonstrates it as God instructs him with his life in obedience. He lays on his side as God instructs him for many days. He turns to the other side also – only as God tells him. Even his food rations are specified by God. He is commanded to use dung to cook his meals. His whole life is a living drama to the nation of Israel of what will occur as Israel will invaded if she does not repent.

Ezekiel 4: 1 You also, son of man, take a brick and lay it before you and inscribe a city on it, even Jerusalem. 2 Then lay siege against it, and build a fort against it, and build a mound against it; set camps and place battering rams against it all around. 3 Moreover take for yourself an iron plate and set it up for a wall of iron between you and the city. And set your face against it so that it is besieged, and lay siege against it. This shall be a sign to the house of Israel.

4 As for you, lie down on your left side and lay the iniquity of the house of Israel upon it. According to the number of the days that you lie on it, you

shall bear their iniquity. 5 For I have laid upon you the years of their iniquity according to the number of the days, three hundred and ninety days. So you shall bear the iniquity of the house of Israel.

6 When you have accomplished them, lie again on your right side, and you shall bear the iniquity of the house of Judah forty days. I have appointed you each day for a year. 7 Therefore you shall set your face toward the siege of Jerusalem, and your arm shall be uncovered, and you shall prophesy against it. 8 I will lay bands upon you, and you shall not turn yourself from one side to another until you have ended the days of your siege.

9 Also take for yourself wheat, and barley, and beans, and lentils, and millet, and spelt, and put them in one vessel and make bread. According to the number of the days that you lie on your side, three hundred and ninety days, you shall eat it. 10 Your food which you shall eat shall be by weight, twenty shekels[a] a day. From time to time you shall eat it. 11 You also shall drink water by measure, the sixth part of a hin.[b] From time to time you shall drink it. 12 You shall eat it as barley cake, having baked it in their sight with dung that comes out of man. 13 Then the Lord said, "Even so the sons of Israel shall eat their defiled bread among the nations where I drive them."

Truly the prophets did not have an easy life as they mostly spoke to people who either did not believe or who did not obey, but some did. There was always a righteous remnant of people who obeyed.

Hosea

Hosea was a prophet of God. God used his life as a living example to Israel also. He was commanded to get a wife who was a prostitute and treat her like a cherished spouse. God wanted to show the wickedness of Israel's sins against God and his mercy towards Israel.

Hosea 1: 2 When the Lord first spoke by Hosea, the Lord said to Hosea: "Go, take for yourself a wife of harlotry and children of harlotry, for the land has committed great harlotry, departing from the Lord." 3 So he went and took Gomer the daughter of Diblaim as a wife. She conceived, and bore him a son.

4 The Lord said to him: "Call his name Jezreel,[a] for in a little while, I will punish the house of Jehu for the blood of Jezreel, and will bring to an end the kingdom of the house of Israel. 5 On that day, I will break the bow of Israel in the Valley of Jezreel."

It is one thing to speak God's words to reprove a sinful nation, but it takes a kind of obedience that is hard to conceive of to literally marry a prostitute and bear children with her. He names his children according to the revelation God gives him about Israel.

It is through the prophesy of Hosea that we understand God's covenant relationship with Israel is as a marriage covenant. God keeps his words and promises to Israel. Even after Hosea's wife leaves him to return to harlotry, God instructs him to go purchase her from the slave trade as her sinful lusts got her into slavery once more. The compassion of God towards sinners is shown in Hosea buying his wife from slave traders and bringing her home and letting her live holy set apart for many days. Once more God uses the prophet to show God's mercy towards sinners who can be changed by God's love. He did it in complete obedience to God.

Hosea 3: 2 So I purchased her for myself for fifteen shekels of silver, and for a homer of barley, and a half homer of barley. 3 Then I said to her, "You will remain with me many days. You will not play the whore, and you will not belong to another man. And also I will be with you."

4 For the children of Israel will remain many days without a king and without a prince, without a sacrifice and without a standing stone, and without an ephod and teraphim. 5 Afterward the children of Israel will return and seek the Lord their God and David their king. They will come in fear to the Lord and to His goodness in the latter days.

I haven given some extreme examples of how God speaks to people and used their lives as examples to the nation they were living in. Prophets may have varying degrees of God using their daily lives to enact truths that affect many people. Some Prophets are called to a church; some to a territory; some to a nation; some to larger territories. God may use all aspects of that prophet's life to show covenant love for his people through his prophet. Prophets are especially chosen to speak for God. They often have situations in their lives that magnify God and warn the people.

New testament prophets mostly encourage, comfort, edify people. Please know though, you need not be a prophet to do these things. They should be aspects of our lives that we desire as much as opportunities to pray for people or to evangelize. Divine encounters can occur for people who believe God and obey him to speak what God would have them to speak. Most often it is words of comfort or encouragement. It will shine like a light because many people who do not know God, live in a different

sort of realm; they cannot see the positive or the good because they are subject to the news and media of their day. They are tossed about by the tides of the world. Worldly news or attractions and affections often ensnare a person who does not know God.
Speaking a positive encouraging message will shine like a light in the darkness.

Matthew 5: 14 "You are the light of the world. A city that is set on a hill cannot be hidden. 15 Neither do men light a candle and put it under a basket, but on a candlestick. And it gives light to all who are in the house. 16 Let your light so shine before men that they may see your good works and glorify your Father who is in heaven.

Chapter 3
End of Chapter questions

1. Explain how God can speak to people. List at least 3 ways.
2. In your own life, how did God speak to you.
3. If there is more than one way God has spoken to you, explain.
4. Explain how you can be sure it is God that has spoken to you.

4 WAYS GOD SPEAKS

Chapter 4

Situations

God may speak to you in situations of your life but do not assume that God brings all situations into your life. If I simply prove to you that God can use situations, you may believe the lie that God teaches you through poverty, illness, or disaster. God can certainly use these things to teach you, but he could also teach you through riches, health and bounty. God may use the situation but never believe the lie that God sends these negative things in your life because he wants to teach you. I like Kenneth Copeland's example of God is not an abuser of his people just as a parent who loves his or her child will not use pain to teach. Certainly, you can learn from those situations but God's covenant with us is clearly indicated as a covenant of blessing.

People who do not know God may say those things about God calling natural disasters "acts of God" as though they are God's will. It is as though someone who really doesn't know you spreads lies about you because they heard someone speaking it. The purpose of this book is not to go in depth of teaching on covenant blessings but if I do not let you know the truth, you may be deceived.

God's covenant with us is clearly stated in Deuteronomy 28 as Moses is given God's covenant with Israel. We are heirs of the promises of God through faith in Jesus Christ. The wealth of the statement is often not regarded by Christians. All of the covenant blessings God made with Moses and Abraham belong to Christians because of what Jesus Christ has done through his death, burial and resurrection as an atonement for our sins. His righteousness is given to those who believe in him and we can inherit the blessings of the covenant.

Galatians 3: 26 You are all sons of God by faith in Christ Jesus. 27 For as many of you as have been baptized into Christ have put on Christ. 28 There is neither Jew nor Greek, there is neither slave nor free, and there is neither male nor female, for you are all one in Christ Jesus. 29 If you are Christ's, then you are Abraham's seed, and heirs according to the promise.

Romans 8: 16 The Spirit Himself bears witness with our spirits that we are the children of God, 17 and if children, then heirs: heirs of God and joint-heirs with Christ, if indeed we suffer with Him, that we may also be glorified with Him.

Deuteronomy 28: 3 You will be blessed in the city and blessed in the field.

4 Your offspring will be blessed, and the produce of your ground, and the offspring of your livestock, the increase of your herd and the flocks of your sheep.

5 Your basket and your kneading bowl will be blessed.

6 You will be blessed when you come in and blessed when you go out.

7 The Lord will cause your enemies who rise up against you to be defeated before you; they will come out against you one way and flee before you seven ways.

8 The Lord will command the blessing on you in your barns and in all that you set your hand to do, and He will bless you in the land which the Lord your God is giving you.

9 The Lord will establish you as a holy people to Himself, just as He swore to you, if you will keep the commandments of the Lord your God and walk in His ways. 10 All people of the earth shall see that you are called by the name of the Lord, and they shall be afraid of you. 11 The Lord will make you overflow in prosperity, in the offspring of your body, in the offspring of your livestock, and in the produce of your ground, in the land which the Lord swore to your fathers to give you.

12 The Lord will open up to you His good treasure, the heavens, to give the rain to your land in its season and to bless all the work of your hand. You will lend to many nations, but you will not borrow. 13 The Lord will make you the head and not the tail; you will only be above and you will not be beneath, if you listen to the commandments of the Lord your God, which I am commanding you today, to observe and to do them. 14 Also, you shall not turn aside from any of the words which I am commanding you today, to the right hand or to the left, to go after other gods to serve them.

Because God's inheritance in Jesus Christ, we are heirs of the promises of God to Israel. There are some specific prophecies about Israel as a people but clearly Christians have been made one with Jews in Messiah Jesus Christ. We can live long, prosperous, abundant lives because of out faith in Jesus. God will not use things contrary to His covenant with us on purpose. He can use those things, but He is not the author of those things. The truth is we live in a world where Adam and Eve sinned against God and the consequences of sin is death.

Romans 6: 23 For the wages of sin is death, but the gift of God is eternal life through Jesus Christ our Lord.

Through Jesus Christ we have redemption and restoration with God. We are made joint heirs with Jesus of all of the covenant blessings of Israel.

Ephesians 1: 7 In Him we have redemption through His blood and the forgiveness of sins according to the riches of His grace, 8 which He lavished on us in all wisdom and insight, 9 making known to us the mystery of His will, according to His good pleasure, which He purposed in Himself, 10 as a plan for the fullness of time, to unite all things in Christ, which are in heaven and on earth.

Jesus righteousness imparted to us gives us access to God but also to the blessings of the covenants. We who were not a people, are made one with the chosen of God – Israel. God has done a miraculous thing in giving us access to Himself and the covenant blessings.

2 Peter 2: 9 But you are a chosen race, a royal priesthood, a holy nation, a people for God's own possession, so that you may declare the goodness of Him who has called you out of darkness into His marvelous light.10 In times past, you were not a people, but now you are the people of God. You had not received mercy, but now you have received mercy.

Galatians 3: 26 You are all sons of God by faith in Christ Jesus. 27 For as many of you as have been baptized into Christ have put on Christ. 28 There is neither Jew nor Greek, there is neither slave nor free, and there is neither male nor female, for you are all one in Christ Jesus. 29 If you are Christ's, then you are Abraham's seed, and heirs according to the promise.

We are all included as part of God's chosen people through the blood of Jesus Christ. No longer are we considered by our earthly heritage. We are direct descendants of Abraham, by faith in Jesus.

If you were not raised as a Christian

If you were not raised in a Christian family, the good news is that you are adopted into the family of God. Jesus Christ adopts you. I give my brief testimony here hoping that you will know that any person can be engrafted into Christ. The Holy Spirit does the transformation. God Himself made the way. It is all of Christ. It is only of us, to obey the promptings of the Holy Spirit and yield our lives to God.

Ephesians 1: 5 He predestined us to adoption as sons to Himself through Jesus Christ according to the good pleasure of His will, 6 to the praise of the glory of His grace which He graciously bestowed on us in the Beloved.

Towards the light

I would describe my relationship with God as moving towards the light. I was not raised in a Christian home. I had some Vacation Bible school at the age of 5. I also had several Bible studies with Jehovah Witnesses as a child. The Hollywood Christian movies were the extent of Christianity in my life. As soon as I received Christ at the age of 21, I felt as though a huge heavy weight was literally taken off of me. I felt light. I felt peace. I felt joy. I realized I had experienced a transformation. I knew I was not the same. Life was in me. I started viewing life differently. I started viewing people differently. My whole perspective had changed.

At first my only Christian companionship was the person who lead me to Christ's family. After I began going to church, I started learning where the books of the Bible were. I started learning Biblical stories and parables and teachings I had never studied. Knowledge brought me insight and perspective.

I started experiencing the sacraments of the Christian faith in a deep spiritual way. I was being transformed from glory to glory in my experience with God. I began to see myself as God's design rather than just a person. I realized He lovingly created me and placed me in my mother's womb (Psalm 139). I began to make Christian friends at Church and my life became so filled with joy that I would honestly say before I had become a Christian I wouldn't have believed it (the joy) were possible on earth. The gospel of Christ, the New Covenant of Jesus is I more awesome and more abundant than any person can express with words. Jesus came to bring us life and life more abundant than we ever could imagine.

John 10: 10 The thief does not come, except to steal and kill and destroy. I came that they may have life, and that they may have it more abundantly.

Jesus came to bring us life more abundant than what we had ever known. What that means is that He reveals all aspects of life to the new Christian so that the person is no longer a stranger but is made a covenant believer who inherits all the blessings of the Covenants of God.

Learning to live a Godly life

I had to learn all things concerned with being a Christian. That included prayer, praise, serving, worshipping, giving, receiving, living holy, running to God, repentance etc. The point is that with the Holy Spirit living on the inside of you, you can learn the lifestyle of a Christian and you can be more effective and more joyful than if you just got saved but didn't pursue God. As that is going on, not separately from your life but through it, because The Holy Spirit is the most awesome teacher anyone could ever have. The Holy Spirit, is God – not a servant, not an angel, not a lesser being, but almighty God living on the inside of you.

That means if God is with you, He can use all aspects of your life to teach you. If you truly desire God, you will be praying, O God change me- so I am more like you. I spent several years at every altar call in the first church I went to. I would mostly cry and ask God to change me. I mostly realized that I wasn't living the scripture because I didn't even know about it.

Knowing the love of God by experience compels you to serve and honour God. It is his mercy towards us that draws us even closer. It is only because of His love towards us that we can know Him. It is this same agape love towards us that draws us like a magnet that draws bits of metal towards itself.

The Holy Spirit: God

The Holy Spirit living inside of Christians is God present with us continuously. The presence of God within a human being is miracle in itself. God cannot tolerate sin. He hates it. That means man and God were separated until Jesus Christ died for our sins so that anyone who believes in Jesus could be saved: cleansed by Jesus, made holy, given access to the presence of God. As we first confess with our mouths that we believe Jesus gave us life for us so that we could have eternal life, the Holy Spirit comes to dwell on the inside of us. Holy God living in an human body, transforming us from the inside of us as our teacher, helper, comforter, friend.

John 14: 17 the Spirit of truth, whom the world cannot receive, for it does not see Him, neither does it know Him. But you know Him, for He lives with you, and will be in you. 18 I will not leave you fatherless. I will come to you. 19 Yet a little while and the world will see Me no more. But you will see Me. Because I live, you will live also.

John 14: 25 "I have spoken these things to you while I am still with you. 26 But the Counselor, the Holy Spirit, whom the Father will send in My name, will teach you everything and remind you of all that I told you. 27 Peace I leave with you. My peace I give to you. Not as the world gives do I give to you. Let not your heart be troubled, neither let it be afraid.

What I am talking about is that God living on the inside of you, even if you had never known God or the things of God can totally transform you so that you become a covenant believer. You know that you know that God is with you and that His love towards you is beyond all earthly love or even the closest human relationship love. Once God resides in you, you will most certainly know it. It is not like some man-made religion where people offer sacrifices but do not communicate with God directly. The Holy Spirit bears witness with our spirits that He is in us and that we belong to Him. That means we know that we know God is with us, living in us. Just as sure as you know when there is someone talking to you in the physical realm, that is how certain you are when the Holy Spirit is talking to your spirit.

Romans 8: 37 No, in all these things we are more than conquerors through Him who loved us. 38 For I am persuaded that neither death nor life, neither angels nor principalities nor powers, neither things present nor things to come, 39 neither height nor depth, nor any other created thing, shall be able to separate us from the love of God, which is in Christ Jesus our Lord.

Obeying the promptings of the Holy Spirit

At first it is like learning about a new friend. As the Holy Spirit directs you, there will be promptings in your spirit that effect you such as "pray for that person" or "throw that out" or "turn that off; it is no good for you." As a parent would teach a child about things dangerous to him or her, God teaches us about things that are pleasing to Him and also things that are not pleasing to Him. At first, I didn't realize that all the things that are not pleasing to God, are things not good for me either. It took prompting from the Holy Spirit and learning to occur so that I understood and believe that God's Word is the best plan for myself and all people. If we would align with God's word, our lives would be transformed. Our lives would be blessed. I mean all areas of life not only church or religion. God can prosper a person in career, home, family, relationships, ministry etc. All of it is contingent on living the Word of God as a life choice. You choose it the day you accept Jesus as Saviour, but you also choose it every day of your life for all your life long.

Learning to discern

Mostly in that first year of my salvation, my relationship with God was developing. I began to learn what it was like to hear God speaking to me. I began to learn the scriptures. I prayed knowing God heard me. I began focussing on God rather than on anything or anyone else. I knew that there was a joyful life beyond what I had ever known living the light of God's covenant blessings. I would experience it at Church. I desired it in all parts of my life, not just at Church. I knew it was superior to anything I had ever known. I desired it more than anything else.

I began learning about God by taking classes at Church and by listening to Christian media and watching Christian Television. It's hard to explain how refreshing it was to me. A person who never knew the darkness cannot fully comprehend the beauty of the light. I knew there was nothing I wanted of the unsaved me. I gave myself to God completely. I did it not just once, but repeatedly. God was always merciful towards me. The Holy Spirit corrected me. The Holy Spirit lead me. My life choices were based on my new Christian identity.

Romans 8: 5 For those who live according to the flesh set their minds on the things of the flesh, but those who live according to the Spirit, the things of the Spirit. 6 To be carnally minded is death, but to be spiritually minded is life and peace, 7 for the carnal mind is hostile toward God, for it is not subject to the law of God, nor indeed can it be, 8 and those who are in the flesh cannot please God.

Romans 8: 9 You, however, are not in the flesh but in the Spirit, if indeed the Spirit of God lives in you. Now if any man does not have the Spirit of Christ, he does not belong to Him. 10 And if Christ is in you, though the body is dead because of sin, the Spirit is alive because of righteousness. 11 But if the Spirit of Him who raised Jesus from the dead lives in you, He who raised Christ from the dead will also give life to your mortal bodies through His Spirit that lives in you.

I give my brief testimony or part of it, in case maybe you were not raised in a Christian home or you think that it is not possible for one who does not have a Christian heritage to live an abundant life. It is not like a country club where people of prestige are born into the wealthiest, famous families. Anybody who believes in Jesus Christ can be changed so that he or she takes his or her identity from God: the blessings of Abraham become your blessings through faith in Jesus Christ. You don't do it yourself. It is you submitting to the Holy Spirit that changes you. You inherit the blessings because God is merciful, generous, compassionate, giving.

Bering transformed

It is your human will aligning with God's Word teaching you. He only brings things to you that need to be changed, as you have the faith and mercy to accept it. A person rarely realizes things from a divine perspective unless God shows him or her. Literally pray that God would help you to see things from a divine perspective. The truth is that although people are sinful, born with the original sin of Adam, with iniquities inherited from relatives, with bad habits because of poor life choices, God sees Christians through the blood of Jesus Christ; He sees us saved and made Holy by Jesus. He is omniscient. He sees us past, present and future. He sees the blood of Jesus applied to our lives; He sees what we can become with His mercy. God sees the best characteristics in us and helps us to develop those very traits that are characteristics of the Holy Spirit.

The blessings of the Mosaic Covenant become yours through faith in Jesus Christ. You realize you do have a godly heritage – it is the saints who have lived before you. It is all the Christian Church in the earth. You are a member of the body of Christ. Your importance is magnified by the one who saved you and placed you as part of His Body in the earth, The Body of Christ is a spiritual force in the earth. The Body of Christ is all Christians who truly believe in Jesus.

1 Corinthians 12: 25 so that there should be no division in the body, but that the parts should have the same care for one another. 26 If one part suffers, all the parts suffer with it, and if one part is honored, all the parts rejoice with it.

27 Now you are the body of Christ and members individually.

The love

Surely each person that knows salvation can tell of the love of God towards him or her. Truly someone who encounters Jesus Christ will know the overwhelming sense of his love towards us. The agape love if God is without condition. He loved us because He is love. He not only has the quality of love, but He is the essence of love. Once a person knows true agape love, he or she will want to share Christ with others. The love of God fills us completely and compels us to share Christ with others. It surpasses all earthly love: friendship or passion. God is love.

1 John 1: 7 Beloved, let us love one another, for love is of God, and everyone who loves is born of God and knows God. 8 Anyone who does not love does not know God, for God is love. 9 In this way the love of God was revealed to us, that God sent His only begotten Son into the world, that we might live through Him. 10 In this is love: not that we loved God, but that He loved us and sent His Son to be the atoning sacrifice for our sins.

Experiencing the love of God will transform us so that His love becomes part of us. We become like him and love others with more than human love. It is the kind of love that makes no sense. Christians should not only love each other, but our love for all people should be a strong aspect of our lives. We should care about the people we meet even if we never see them again. We should respect all people, showing mercy and compassion towards them.

Luke 6: 30 Give to everyone who asks of you. And of him who takes away your goods, do not ask for them back. 31 Do unto others as you would have others do unto you.

Loving God is a commandment of Jehovah. Loving people is a commandment of Jesus. They are not separate. A person who truly loves God with all his or her being will certainly love others with the love of God within. Love is not just a quality. It is an essential aspect of God's character. Since He lives in us and through us, we will be moved by it caring for others.

Deuteronomy 6: 4 Hear, O Israel: The Lord is our God. The Lord is one! 5 And you shall love the Lord your God with all your heart and with all your soul and with all your might.

John 13: 34 "A new commandment I give to you, that you love one another, even as I have loved you, that you also love one another. 35 By this all men will know that you are My disciples, if you have love for one another."

Once of the first changes in me after I became a Christian is that I began loving people. I would say I always cared about people but after I became a Christian, I truly started loving them by wanting to give to them and certainly introduce them to Jesus Christ. I became less focussed on me and more Christ centered. Also, being Christ centered means caring about people the way Christ cares about people.

God loved us before we knew Him

It is essential not only to grasp these truths yourself but to share them with others who do not yet know Christ. I believe if people truly knew how much God loved them, they would consider knowing Him. Sharing His love towards them is an essential aspect of witnessing.

1 John 4: 19 We love because he first loved us.

Ephesians 1: 4 For he chose us in him before the creation of the world to be holy and blameless in his sight. In love 5 he[b] predestined us for adoption to sonship[c] through Jesus Christ, in accordance with his pleasure and will—

Unconditional love

The agape love of God is such that it can not be explained with human terms or comparisons. It is beyond what our language can describe. It is overwhelming; the height, depth, width, and length are without end.

A new Christian will feel an overwhelming sense of God's love towards them. It goes beyond all earthy description. It is eternal unconditional love. We don't earn it; we can't buy it. It is a gift to those who will believe on Christ Jesus.

Ephesians 3: 17 and that Christ may dwell in your hearts through faith; that you, being rooted and grounded in love, 18 may be able to comprehend with all saints what is the breadth and length and depth and height, 19 and to know the love of Christ which surpasses knowledge; that you may be filled with all the fullness of God.

The magnetic pull of Divine Love

Whether or not you were raised in a Christian home, God's mercy was pulling you towards Himself before you ever confessed Him as Saviour. There were opportunities throughout your life God drew you towards Himself. As we pray for non-Christians, that God would shine the light of Christ in their hearts so that they would receive Jesus as Saviour and Lord, there are angels released or assigned to draw the people. Also, there are people released who would share Christ with them. I myself had several occasions to receive Jesus. There were people – not many but several who gave me brief discussion about Jesus. I did not know the full truth of the gospel of salvation, healing and deliverance until I received Jesus at the age of 21.

It was God's mercy pulling me all throughout my life. I felt like I wanted to know God but didn't know where to find Him. As I searched through Eastern Religions and mysticism, I was further from the truth and no closer to knowing God. Finally, with the simplicity of a servant of God who spoke prophetically (I knew he was speaking God's words because only God and I knew about it – but I didn't know it was called prophecy) into my life at the exact moment my heart was soft, willing to receive God's salvation.

Think prayerfully over your own life about the moments where you knew someone was talking to you about God. Each of those opportunities was God's mercy drawing you closer. This should not only encourage us that God loved us before we loved Him. God was drawing us before we were seeking Hi;, it should also cause us to pray for people who do not yet know Christ. As we pray, God releases mercy towards that person.

The miracle of salvation

The miracle of our own salvation should compel us to share Christ with others. Knowing that God can reach anyone, knowing that God can do all things, knowing that God's mercy is towards all people, should compel us to share our testimonies or stories of what God has done for us with others.

I am completely supportive of street evangelism and organized efforts to win people to Christ. These should be our corporate goals as a Church. There also private one on one opportunities that God may give us talking to someone that we may never see again or meet again. For instance, you may be sitting talking to someone on a train or bus or plane. You may be standing in line at a bank. You may be simply walking and pass a stranger on the street. These simple, ordinary life moments that are once in a lifetime opportunity may very well be God's mercy reaching towards those individuals through us should be obey the Holy Spirit's promptings.

Even though we are as ordinary people going about normal life on earth, God is living in us and cares about all people (and animals) around us. God may speak to us. There are different types of promptings that I myself have experienced. There is an impression. The impression is like a nudge from a friend to let you know something personal and to help you. It could be an inner voice, speaking directions to you. It could be a scripture that comes to you. There are others who have heard the audible voice of God. I have only experienced inner witnessing – God speaking directly to my spirit. If we will obey, how it could impact the world with deeds of kindness and charitable acts.

The Word of God

God always keeps his word. He always answers our prayers when our prayers align with the Word of God. God never goes contrary to his Word. There is a movie by the Title of Bruce almighty. It is a funny movie about a person who God gives ultimate power to. At first, he enjoys using the power to help himself. Later though he starts getting thousands of people praying and he wants to help them, so he says yes to all their prayer requests. What happens is that everyone who bought a ticket for the lottery, won the lottery. They won under a dollar. It is humorous but also important that we understand God doesn't simply say yes to everything we pray.

God keeps His word as the standard by which He answers prayer. God will not violate His own commandments and He will not violate a person's human will. Once we grasp the truth of it, God's Word is His will for us and it is the best possible choice for us so that we can live long, prosperous, enjoyable lives, we will study the Word of God more than anything else. We will desire to know what God's Word says not just as an interest but because it directly affects our lives and can lead us in truth. God's Word is our joy, our victory, our life. It is important that we both know the Word of God and use it as the standards in making all decisions.

Joshua 1: 7 Be strong and very courageous, in order to act carefully in accordance with all the law that My servant Moses commanded you. Do not turn aside from it to the right or the left, so that you may succeed wherever you go. 8 This Book of the Law must not depart from your mouth. Meditate on it day and night so that you may act carefully according to all that is written in it. For then you will make your way successful, and you will be wise. 9 Have not I commanded you? Be strong and courageous.

Do not be afraid or dismayed, for the Lord your God is with you wherever you go."

We may quote a scripture or paraphrase a scripture to someone we meet. That person may be impacted by it eternally. God's Word never returns void. It always accomplishes what it is sent to do. We don't have to find a way for God's Word to impact a person; all we do is be obedient to God's promptings so that God can use us. It is like we are messengers we are always ready to bring good news to people. We are ministers or ambassadors for Christ. We share the things God quickens to us. Please realize the more of God's Word that you know, the more you will be able to share with others. Reading the Word of God is not only good to build up our own selves in the faith but also so that we can sow the word of God into others lives.

Isaiah 55: 11 so shall My word be that goes forth from My mouth;
   it shall not return to Me void,
but it shall accomplish that which I please,
   and it shall prosper in the thing for which I sent it.

A simple verse or scripture or kind words spoken to a person can bring hope or light into that person's life. Often there is negative news that is in the media or in the conversations of many people. We Christians are bearers of the good news of Jesus Christ. We should always be ready to encourage someone or to speak some positive word to someone. Consider it sowing into the kingdom of God. Often a kind deed, such as helping someone carry groceries or giving a ride to someone even though it is our of our normal way, or helping a child – simple things, ordinary things, although they are not outwardly "big" or noteworthy are real ways we can show the love of God for people. It will begin to release joy in you because you know you are doing something that God cares about.

Often people want God to do something for them. They seek God always wanting to receive from Him. As you realize his love and compassion towards you, you really love God and desire to care about the things He cares about. You will literally start praying "God help me to care about what you care about." That will include people and animals. We will begin to view the world as a place to impart or make a difference rather than simply a place for us to take from. It becomes a stewardship issue in our lives. You realize that all the people and creatures in your life are there and you if you can help someone, you will do it. You will begin serving and giving from the love of God that is in you. The more you press into God, the more you become like Him. You more you will love people with a love that cannot be understood in earthly terms because it is the Agape love of God loving through you.

Should you grasp the love of God toward you that is unconditional and eternal, you will never be the same. You will be overwhelmed by his love and the riches of the knowledge of his glory. The glory of God is eternal. There is no way of measuring it. Once you experience His true love, you will never be the same.

Ephesians 1: 15 Therefore I also, after hearing of your faith in the Lord Jesus and your love toward all the saints, 16 do not cease giving thanks for you, mentioning you in my prayers, 17 so that the God of our Lord Jesus Christ, the Father of glory, may give you the Spirit of wisdom and revelation in the knowledge of Him, 18 that the eyes of your understanding may be enlightened, that you may know what is the hope of His calling and what are the riches of the glory of His inheritance among the saints, 19 and what is the surpassing greatness of His power toward us who believe, according to the working of His mighty power, 20 which He performed in Christ when He raised Him from the dead and seated Him at His own right hand in the heavenly places, 21 far above all principalities, and power, and might, and dominion, and every name that is named, not only in this age but also in that which is to come.

I've given scripture on the love of God. I've tried to describe the awesomeness of it The only way to get more revelation of it is to literally pray "God – give me light – give me revelation of your love. " Pray that you may be a vessel God can use to show His love towards people and animals.

Chapter 4
End of chapter questions

1. Give specific examples of God prompting you to speak to someone, pray for someone and or speak words of encouragement to someone.
2. Explain how you keep your attitude humble and your character godly.
3. If you have not considered praying for God to develop your godly character by the fruit of the Spirit, start praying for the fruit specifically.
4. In your daily prayer, include praying and receiving spiritual growth in areas of your character.
5. Prayerfully ask God to reveal scriptures to you that can build you up in your character.

THE ALTAR

Chapter 5

We first know about an altar of sacrifice as it described in Genesis when both Cain and Abel offer sacrifices to God to thank Him for providing for them (Genesis 4). Afterwards, altars are described as places to give worship – including offerings or sacrifices of animals. There are some instances in scripture where people offer themselves to God. They are not unrelated because a person who would freely offer himself to God would also offer animals or sacrifice. The altar is also a place of first knowing God. The person offers himself as an offering. The person makes a destiny decision that changes his or her life. The altar could be associated with a certain place, but it also relates to an inner space of spirit that has given to God. There were places where God revealed himself to people and they made altars there. They were places of worship.

Jacob
Genesis 35: 7 There he built an altar, and he called the place El Bethel,[a] because it was there that God revealed himself to him when he was fleeing from his brother.

Jacob associates the place with God. The place itself is emphasized as a place to meet with God.

Isaac Genesis 26: 23 From there he went up to Beersheba. 24 That night the Lord appeared to him and said, "I am the God of your father Abraham. Do not be afraid, for I am with you; I will bless you and will increase the number of your descendants for the sake of my servant Abraham."

25 Isaac built an altar there and called on the name of the Lord. There he pitched his tent, and there his servants dug a well.

Once more the place is identified with God. Isaac believed God lead him to the place and finally after digging so many wells, finally there was one well and there was peace. He honours the Lord by calling it the place where God has made room for us.

Moses

Exodus 17: 15 Moses built an altar and called it The Lord is my Banner. 16 He said, "Because hands were lifted up against[c] the throne of the Lord,[d] the Lord will be at war against the Amalekites from generation to generation."

Once more the place itself is honoured because God helped Israel to defeat the Amalekites and God promises that He himself will fight against them. Because of God's word, Moses honours the LORD there and makes an altar.

God gives Moses instructions

God gave Moses specific instructions of worship including all aspects of it including the altar and offering of sacrifices. Judaism began with Jehovah and was given to Moses who taught it to the people. God also gives specific instruction on how to build an altar to God.

God gave Moses instructions about building an altar to Jehovah. It is essential that it not be crafted or fashioned by man. It was simple. There are stones assembled. The purpose for simplicity is so that man will not trust in his craftsmanship or talent believing falsely that it could earn him a closer place to God. God does not honour it because of the beauty of the altar itself but by the sincerity of the heart offering a gift.

After God gave the commandments to Moses and Israel, animal sacrifices were offered for many purposes. They offered sacrifices for sins, but also for special mercy and thanksgiving. Aaron's family were chosen by God to offer sacrifices and keep the tabernacle of the wilderness, the dwelling place of God with Israel. There was an outer court, an inner holy place and the holy of holies an inner place that held the ark of the covenant with the presence of God. God specifically instructed Moses how it was to be constructed.

Exodus 20: 24 "'Make an altar of earth for me and sacrifice on it your burnt offerings and fellowship offerings, your sheep and goats and your cattle. Wherever I cause my name to be honored, I will come to you and bless you. 25 If you make an altar of stones for me, do not build it with dressed stones, for you will defile it if you use a tool on it. 26 And do not go up to my altar on steps, or your private parts may be exposed.'

The altar is giving

The altar of the believer is a point of offering to God something eternal. It is not simply giving an animal sacrifice. It is totally relevant today because even though we do not have a physical temple to offer sacrifices as the Israelites had, we do offer sacrifice. It includes giving of tithes and offerings to the church as unto God. It is more than physical giving. It is a spiritual type of giving of worship acknowledging God.

The first giving of yourself to God occurs at salvation, but it should continue regularly as an expression of will. There should be a continuous giving of self in worship. I learned about making an altar in the churches I was a part of. Often if a prophecy came in church people would go kneel at the altar in church or make an altar at their seats. I learned that when God's Spirit was moving on me, whether in the congregation or at home, I should kneel and give myself to God. The way I would most describe it is as a strong compulsion to give myself to God. Often, I would pray in tongues and receive spiritual life. It was a constant giving of myself. I do it regularly also now. It is living in a place of giving yourself to God wholly. The worshipper himself or herself becomes a willing sacrifice.

1 Thessalonians 5: 23 May the very God of peace sanctify you completely. And I pray to God that your whole spirit, soul, and body be preserved blameless unto the coming of our Lord Jesus Christ.

Because Jesus lives within us in the person of the Holy Spirit, there is an inner giving of our being by an act of human will – we willfully give ourselves to God. It is true worship; the worshippers offer: his or her life to God completely. It means you offer thanksgiving, praise and worship but also that you are willing to obey the Holy Spirit's leading. By praying this type of giving of prayer, a person can be used by God. The person is willing.

Seeking, worshipping, praising, praying, listening, living

Romans 12 : 1 I urge you therefore, brothers, by the mercies of God, that you present your bodies as a living sacrifice, holy, and acceptable to God, which is your reasonable service of worship. 2 Do not be conformed to this world, but be transformed by the renewing of your mind, that you may prove what is the good and acceptable and perfect will of God.

There could be a song that cause one to express passion or love for God. There could be a scripture read or a preached word that touches the believer's heart. The response of the believer is that he or she knows God is drawing him or her nearer. By willingly acknowledging God's presence, the person gives himself or herself fresh to God. Sometimes, God may answer a prayer in a miraculous way. Sometimes, God will speak a word and seal it upon the believer's heart. Other times it is simply a surrendering of the worshipper in a new way. The person may not have revelation of the reason for the fresh yielding at the moment, but it may be remembered later as a place of decision to obey God.

The altar is a place – and that place can be anywhere the believer is. It is a moment where there is a decision made to pursue God, to choose God over anything or anyone else. It is an expression of devotion to God. The believer will remember it as a place and a season of life. The truth is that our relationship with God is a constant deciding to live and serve God each day of our lives. Those special altar moments are life changing because it is a drawing of the Creator to the creature. We draw close to Him and it is significant to our lives on earth and in the spiritual realm.

Joshua 1: 9 Have not I commanded you? Be strong and courageous. Do not be afraid or dismayed, for the Lord your God is with you wherever you go."

The altar call may be lead by a minister in church or by the direct leading of the Holy Spirit. There is a strong inner prompting to serve God, to seek God fresh. The experience itself may be of some specific thing the person has been praying about or it can be without known reason. It is not the same for any two people, although sometimes husband and wife pray together about something important.

An altar call has eternal implications. The decisions made there can directly affect the worshipper's present and future life on earth. There is also spiritual significance to the offering.

At some altar calls, people are physically healed immediately. At some altar calls people are baptized in the Holy Spirit with the evidence of speaking in other tongues. At some altar calls, people repent and turn to God with fresh consecration. At others, people agree with God concerning a preached word to be applied to his or her family and life. The person can receive from God salvation, healing, deliverance, boldness etc. It is a special duration that draws a person close to God. Should the person willfully decide to embrace God's drawing, the person will receive blessing beyond what words alone can describe. There will be an experience with God, a closeness and a sealing of relationship with God concerning the things of earth.

When these occasions come to me in my home, I like to honour the LORD by taking communion. It is a remembering of the blood covenant of Jesus Christ. It is an acceptance of God's provision once and for always. Jesus Christ took our place as the only Holy sacrifice so that should be believe in Him, we have eternal life. It is not simply a ritual. It is celebrating the LORD's covenant with us. We on purpose remember Jesus sacrifice for us. It is a way of honouring God and keeping covenant with Him.

1 Corinthians 11: 23 I have received of the Lord that which I delivered to you: that the Lord Jesus, on the night in which He was betrayed, took bread. 24 When He had given thanks, He broke it and said, "Take and eat. This is My body which is broken for you. Do this in remembrance of Me."[a] 25 In the same manner He took the cup after He had supper, saying, "This cup is the new covenant in My blood. Do this, as often as you drink it, in remembrance of Me."[b] 26 As often as you eat this bread and drink this cup, you proclaim the Lord's death until He comes.

The altar call is not simply everyone obeying the leader or the pastor. It is an inward witness of the Holy Spirit knowing you are doing the right thing as the Holy Spirit beckons you to come close. Your obedience to God is honouring God. It will most certainly affect your life. There may be someone praying for you at the altar or you may pray on your own with God's Spirit's leading. During these experiences the believer will often experience a strong presence of the Holy Spirit. It is in these decisions of obedience that a believer is strengthened, and his faith renewed.

A person's personal life with God directly affects his or her witnessing to others about God. When believers are filled with God's Holy presence and strengthened in their faith, they will want to share Christ with everyone around them. The person will naturally speak of God because He is most important to him or her. It will affect our conversation; it will affect our relationships. We will want others to know the goodness of God. Also, the people will automatically desire to pray for others. You will start serving others and giving – the believers' lives become the scripture; we become as living epistles. It is living the commandments rather than just memorizing them.

Matthew 22: 37 Jesus said to him, " 'You shall love the Lord your God with all your heart, and with all your soul, and with all your mind.'[c] 38 This is the first and great commandment. 39 And the second is like it: 'You shall love your neighbor as yourself.'[d] 40 On these two commandments hang all the Law and the Prophets."

The more a person is praying, encountering the true living God, the more the person is changed to become more Christ like in character. The person will begin to love people because he will begin to see them as God sees them. The worshipper will begin to care for others and to give, and to serve, whether in church or in the community because he knows God is the only true way for eternal life as well as peace, prosperity or joy in this life. Often, the person will be overwhelmed by love for all types of people and nations as well as people they know.

A person who is yielded to God daily is someone God can use. God desires someone willing as well as obedient. One sure way God uses people is in intercessory prayer. The person will often start praying for people because they know God hears and answers prayers and that it can affect the spiritual world as well as the natural world.

Ephesians 6: 18 Pray in the Spirit always with all kinds of prayer and supplication. To that end be alert with all perseverance and supplication for all the saints.

Instruction

If you are a new Christian or get a strong desire to go to the altar at church or feel God drawing you in your home and you do not know what to do, please consider these instructions.

1. Stop whatever you were going to do and seek the LORD. It may not always be possible because it could occur in your workplace or in the car driving etc. First, choose to draw close to God and as soon as you can speak to God offering yourself saying "Here I am God. Please speak to your servant. I give myself to you." It doesn't have to be those exact words, but the meaning should be the same. You are willing. You are obedient, and you offer yourself – all within your earthly sphere of authority to God.

2. It could last long, or it could be brief. It is never without reason. If you know what it is about – because God quickens it to your spirit – pray the thing and agree with God. If it is confessing a sin or wrong attitude, do it. It is it is a prompting to pray for someone, do it. If it is a prompting to give or to visit someone, do it. Those acts of obedience can yield rewards beyond what you know in this life. You may never realize the importance of saying yes in those moments until the life to come.

3. Sometimes, something you have been praying about becomes so clear to you during your meeting with God that you know what things you should do. God may quicken a scripture or speak a Word. If you do not experience from the drawing to God – keep

praying about it constantly. Make it a priority. Daniel prayed about such a prompting because of the dreams he had for 3 weeks. He prayed and kept on praying until the answer came.

Matthew 7: 7 "Ask and it will be given to you; seek and you will find; knock and it will be opened to you. 8 For everyone who asks receives, and he who seeks finds, and to him who knocks, it will be opened.

Once you have felt a release in your spirit or an answer has manifested, you will feel a release to go about your life more normally. It could be a short duration. It could be a long duration. God will use those encounters with you to inspire you, comfort you, strengthen you, encourage you and establish you as well as instruct you.

Chapter 5
End of chapter questions

1. Explain your altar call response to salvation. Give your testimony.
2. Explain a significant altar call moment in your life as transformed your life.
3. Explain a recent altar call and what occurred. Consider making daily offerings of yourself as a living, willing, sacrifice to God. Read Isaiah 6. Pray that God would use you to speak His word.

6 OLD COVENANT

Chapter 6
Old Covenant – without the indwelling of God

In the Old testament, the champions of faith had encounters with God. God spoke to them and His Holy Spirit would come upon the prophets and they would prophesy. The Holy Spirit would come upon the Levitical priests and they would worship and praise God.

The presence of God was an event or an occurrence because the people were living with animal sacrifices for sin. Because of the sin of Adam and Eve, man was separate from God and there was not direct communication with God for most people. Animals sacrifices were given as a sign of drawing close to God. The people were desiring to come to God, but they were separated by original sin from direct communication with God. The animal sacrifice covered over the sin to give the person favour with God. Most people did not directly speak with God but rather were taught by the priests or the prophets. God's reaching towards man was in the establishment of the Mosaic covenant. By obeying the commandments and the Levitical laws, the people were living a life of blessing and favour of God. They were promised that God would prosper them, keep them strong and healthy, fruitful and God Himself would defend them.

Deuteronomy 11: 13 It will be, if you will diligently obey My commandments which I am commanding you today, to love the Lord your God, and to serve Him with all your heart and with all your soul, 14 then I will give you the rain of your land in its season, the early rain and the latter rain, that you may gather in your grain and your wine and your oil. 15 I will provide grass in your fields for your livestock, that you may eat and be full.

Deuteronomy 11: 18 Therefore you must fix these words of mine in your heart and in your soul, and bind them as a sign on your hand, so that they may be as frontlets between your eyes. 19 You shall teach them to your children, speaking of them when you sit in your house and when you walk by the way, when you lie down, and when you rise up. 20 You shall write them on the doorposts of your house and on your gates, 21 so that your days and the days of your children may be multiplied in the land which the Lord swore to your fathers to give them, as long as the days of heaven on the earth.

People who wanted a specific answer to pray would often go to a prophet or a seer and make the request. The person would pray and minister to the seeker. The prophets were mostly men but there were some women. Deborah was such a prophet.

Judges 4: 1 Now Deborah, the wife of Lappidoth, was a prophetess. She judged Israel at that time. 5 She would sit under the palm tree of Deborah between Ramah and Bethel in the hill country of Ephraim. The children of Israel would go up to her for her to render judgment.

Moving the sun dial backwards

Asking for a sign from God from God is also known as laying a fleece. It was a way of asking God to prove his promise before it occurred. It was a plea from people who did not know the character of ways of God to confirm God speaking to them. The people who loved God did not have the presence of God or the Word of God. They tried to comprehend the words God spoke to them by asking for signs of confirmation.

Isaiah 38: 1 In those days Hezekiah was mortally ill. And Isaiah the prophet, the son of Amoz, came to him and said to him, "Thus says the Lord: Set your house in order, for you shall die, and not live."

2 Then Hezekiah turned his face toward the wall, and prayed to the Lord, 3 and said, "Remember now, O Lord, I beseech You, how I have walked before You in truth and with a perfect heart, and have done what is good in Your sight." And Hezekiah wept bitterly.

4 Then the word of the Lord came to Isaiah, saying: 5 "Go, and say to Hezekiah, Thus says the Lord, the God of David your father: I have heard your prayer, I have seen your tears. Surely I will add to your days fifteen years. 6 I will deliver you and this city out of the hand of the king of Assyria, and I will defend this city.

7 "This shall be a sign to you from the Lord, that the Lord will do this thing that He has spoken: 8 I will cause the shadow on the sundial, which has gone down with the sun on the sundial of Ahaz, to go back ten steps." So the sun's shadow returned ten steps on the sundial by which it had gone down.Leaving a fleece – Gideon Judges 6: 36 – 40

When God directly spoke with people, often they were not completely sure it was God. Remember they did not have the indwelling presence of God as we do. Such is the instance with Gideon. He was an ordinary farmer. He was going about his regular tasks of threshing wheat when an angel of the LORD appeared and greeted him with a strange greeting.

Judges 6: 11 Now the angel[a] of the Lord came and sat under the oak tree in Ophrah belonging to Joash the Abiezrite. Gideon his son was threshing wheat in a winepress to hide it from the Midianites. 12 The angel of the Lord appeared and said to him, "The Lord is with you, O mighty man of valor."

It was an usual greeting to be called a mighty man of valor because Israel was being oppressed by the Midianites an enemy. Gideon was hiding his winepress to keep it from being taken away. He was an ordinary person. God's angel entered his life that day with an unusual message and a task that would change his life and the lives of all of Israel. Rather than Gideon thank God for this angelic encounter, he complains that God has left them in slavery to their enemy. The angels' words are hard to believe.

God's words to Gideon were tough to believe. Judges 6: 14 Then the Lord turned to him and said, "Go in this strength of yours. Save Israel from the control of Midian. Have I not sent you?"
He wondered how one normal person save all of Israel.

Judges 6: 15 And he said to Him, "O my Lord, how can I save Israel? Indeed my clan is the weakest in Manasseh, and I am the youngest in my father's house."

16 Then the Lord said to him, "But I will be with you, and you will strike the Midianites as one man."

God promised to be with him and to use him to defeat the enemy. Although Gideon heard the words clearly and knew it was an angel of the LORD speaking, although he knew the God of Israel was God, he couldn't believe. He wanted a sign. He wanted some type of proof from God that it was true. The angel disappears into the food offering that Gideon had prepared and Gideon knows surely it was a messenger from God. His first task was to tear down the altar of Baalm a false god. He got some men together and they did it by night. The men of the city wanted to punish Gideon. Joash (Gideon's dad) has a strong word against those who came to kill Gideon. He reminds them that Baal is an idol and if he was a god, he should defend himself.

Because of the tearing down of the altar to Baal, many men gathered with Gideon willing to fight for Israel. Gideon wanted proof that God's words for him to lead Israel to defeat the Midianites was true. He had a sheep skin covering – it was a fleece. He chose it and asked for proof.

Judges 6: 36 Gideon said to God, "If You will use my hands to save Israel, as You have said— 37 I am placing a fleece of wool on the threshing floor. If there is dew on the fleece only and all of the ground remains dry, then I will know that You will save Israel with my hands, as You have said." 38 So it happened. He got up early the next morning and squeezed the fleece. Enough dew poured out of the fleece to fill a bowlful of water.

The sign he asked for was impossible. Only God could do it. The fleece was soaking with water but all the ground around it was dry. Even though it occurred even as he requested, he still requesting another proof.

Judges 6: 39 Then Gideon said to God, "Do not let Your anger burn against me as I speak only one more time. Please let me perform a test with the fleece one more time. Please, let the fleece be the only thing dry, and let there be dew on all of the ground." 40 So God did this during that night. Only the fleece was dry, and the dew was on all the ground.

Although God does exactly as Gideon asks he still has doubts about invading the Midianites. Many people use "praying a fleece" prayers as a way to get an answer from God. Basically, it means, give me proof God that you are speaking to me. Although God will honour each person at his point of faith, He may answer someone by proving himself as He did with Gideon, it is not the most effective way to pray.

First, we are living in the New Covenant of Jesus blood. Jesus cleansed us from all sin as though we never sinned. The Holy Spirit is living inside of believers. The real Holy Spirit of God is dwelling in us. We are the temple of the Holy Spirit. We can directly speak with God. That is the main reason I am writing this book to discuss developing your communication with God. People under the Old Covenant never had such an opportunity. We should know God's voice. We also have the Holy Scriptures – God's Word. The saints in the Old Testament did not have copies of God's Word. Only the Levitical priests had the scriptures. Later it was hand copied by people because there was no printing press.

Life in the new covenant: Jesus our Saviour

We have God's expressed will for our lives. It is possible for all people in the Western world to purchase a copy of the Scriptures in stores. It is harder to get for believers in nations that do not allow freedom of worship, but they do get copies. The Holy Spirit living within us confirms God's will towards us. Our human spirit receives peace, joy, enlightenment as God speaks to us. Also, we can search the scriptures to get exact scriptures on all aspects of human life. Both knowing the person of the Holy Spirit and reading the scriptures and believing them requires faith. Faith in God is necessary to receive from God.

Hebrews 11: 6 And without faith it is impossible to please God, for he who comes to God must believe that He exists and that He is a rewarder of those who diligently seek Him.

Each believer can directly speak to God. Each Christian can read the Bible and learn the truths of God's word for his own life. Living by faith in Jesus is easier than offering animal sacrifices for sin. Even the Levitical priests and the prophets did not have the Holy Presence of God continuously abiding in them. God has done a miraculous thing. Even though we are born with original sin of Adam and Eve, even though there is no righteousness in us, God draws us to Himself and as we accept Jesus as Saviour and LORD, the Holy Spirit comes to live inside our human spirit. We are reconciled to God or made one with God. Even as Abraham believed God and it was counted to him as righteousness, so we also can believe God.

If we do not believe the God who dwells in us, if we do not believe the God whose Word we can read and pray, we are sinning against God. A Christian knows the presence of God. If you don't yet know, you will know because it is God's will for you to have relationship with him. The reason he sent Jesus is so that we could be restored to God. God created us to be in intimate relationship with Him. Christians are in direct communion with God.

Ephesians 2: 19 Now, therefore, you are no longer strangers and foreigners, but are fellow citizens with the saints and members of the household of God,

Ephesians 1: 5 He predestined us to adoption as sons to Himself through Jesus Christ according to the good pleasure of His will, 6 to the praise of the glory of His grace which He graciously bestowed on us in the Beloved. 7 In Him we have redemption through His blood and the forgiveness of sins according to the riches of His grace, 8 which He lavished on us in all wisdom and insight, 9 making known to us the mystery of His will, according to His good pleasure, which He purposed in Himself,

God considers us his family. Even though He is Omnipotent and almighty, He rejoices in speaking with us, teaching us and blessing us. It is something only God could do. He comes in live within us so that we can be in communion with Him.

2 Corinthians 4: 6 For God, who commanded the light to shine out of darkness, has shone in our hearts to give the light of the knowledge of the glory of God in the face of Jesus Christ.

7 But we have this treasure in earthen vessels, the excellency of the power being from God and not from ourselves.

The glory of God inside of humans – this is what makes Christianity different than any other religion. God lives within us. Throughout the ages, God has been reaching towards man with various covenants extending mercy towards us. Finally, in the new covenant we are given complete forgiveness by faith in Jesus Christ. Our sins are cleansed, and we are made holy, all by faith in Jesus Christ.

Colossians 1: 27 To them God would make known what is the glorious riches of this mystery among the nations. It is Christ in you, the hope of glory,

The highest

Jesus Christ is our righteousness. The Word of God is our instruction guide for living. All things that pertain to life are covered in the scriptures. God can and does speak to us. Living by faith in Jesus Christ is the most exciting and joyful life a person could imagine. People are seeking a way to get "high". It usually means escaping reality with drugs or alcohol. If these people could know Jesus, they would realize the pleasures of God are not comparable to any temporary substance high. Living by faith is living in the high calling that God has for our lives. Relationship with God is exciting because whatever God says occurs. God never lies. God can explain things to any person in any profession because He created all of us.

Philippians 3: 14 I press toward the goal to the prize of the high calling of God in Christ Jesus.

People would go to Moses to get answers from God

Because Moses lead Israel out of slavery in Egypt through the wilderness, people knew that Moses was close to God. There were many miracles. The people feared God because they knew He was Holy and they were not. The people went to Moses to be the mediator. They would ask Moses about matters of life and Moses would answer by the wisdom God gave him. It seemed like a solution, but it was not the best solution.

Exodus 18: 15 Then Moses said to his father-in-law, "Because the people come to me to inquire of God. 16 When they have a dispute, it comes to me, and I judge between a man and his neighbor, and I make known the statutes of God and His laws."

Later in the same passage, Jethro speaks wisdom to him to appoint men of wisdom to share the burden of all the people. Moses listens to Jethro's wise advice and more people are used to teach the people God's statutes.

Exodus 18: 19 Now listen to me, I will advise you, and may God be with you: You be a representative for the people to God so that you may bring their disputes to God. 20 And you shall teach them the statutes and laws and shall show them the way in which they must walk and the work that they must do. 21 Moreover, you shall choose out of all the people capable men who fear God, men of truth, hating dishonest gain, and place these men over them, to be rulers of thousands, rulers of hundreds, rulers of fifties, and rulers of tens. 22 Let them judge the people at all times, and let it be that every difficult matter they shall bring to you, but every small matter they shall judge, so that it will be easier for you, and they will bear the burden with you. 23 If you shall do this thing and God commands you so, then you will be able to endure, and all these people also will go to their place in peace."

The Tabernacle of Moses: Moses and Aaron as intercessors

More than once, Moses and Aaron pray that God will forgive Israel for their sins so that God's judgement would not come on them. Moses and Aaron feel a love towards Israel that is the true love of shepherds or pastors for their congregation. Although they do not condone sin and will not tolerate it, they plead for mercy for the people who are Moses and Aaron intercede for Israel, so the plagues would be stopped. They are as mediators – they stand in the place of intercessor for Israel. They speak God's words to the people of Israel.

Numbers 16: 46 Moses said to Aaron, "Take a censer and put fire in it from off the altar, and put in incense, and go quickly to the assembly, and make an atonement for them, because wrath has gone out from the Lord. The plague has begun." 47 Aaron took it as Moses commanded and ran into the midst of the assembly, where the plague had begun among the people. He put in incense and made an atonement for the people. 48 He stood between the dead and the living, and the plague was stopped.

Jesus corrected those who asked for a sign

Jesus spoke correcting Pharisees who desired a sign from Jesus that he had authority to speak. They were "tempting God" because they knew of the miracles Jesus had done in feeding 4, 000 people but did not believe. There are people who can witness miracles, even receive a miracle from God but their hearts are not right with God; they do not believe. The rebuke that Jesus gives to them is not because they sincerely want to believe. It is because although Jesus the Messiah had come and was in their midst, they did not believe. The ultimate sign of Jesus dying and being resurrected occurred, but many did not believe.

Matthew 16: 4 A wicked and adulterous generation seeks for a sign, but no sign shall be given to it except the sign of the prophet Jonah." So He left them and departed.

Jesus was not referring to a literal repeat of the miracle of Jonah. He used it as a metaphor for what would occur with his life, death, burial and resurrection from the dead. Jesus was prophesying. The disciples did not understand but later they understood.

A measure of faith

Jesus taught that each person has a measure of faith and that even a small seed of faith is mighty and can move a mountain. It is not the size of the faith but the application of it. Faith is substance of things hoped for (Hebrews 11:1) and of evidence not yet seen. Using the measure of faith, one has can lead to miracles. Faith is a spiritual substance. No one can receive anything from God without it. All people have a measure of it.

Matthew 17: 20 Jesus said to them, "Because of your unbelief. For truly I say to you, if you have faith as a grain of mustard seed, you will say to this mountain, 'Move from here to there,' and it will move. And nothing will be impossible for you.

All things are possible

All things are possible as the believer uses faith. You only learn to release your faith as you hear God's word. Faith comes by hearing and hearing the word of God (Romans 10: 17) As a believer hears God word with his ears, it releases faith in his inner being. The more of the Word of God that you hear, the more you will build up your faith.

Hebrews 11: 6 And without faith it is impossible to please God, for he who comes to God must believe that He exists and that He is a rewarder of those who diligently seek Him.

God gives us the encouragement to ask of things we desire

Jesus instructed his disciples that if they would ask God in faith, they would receive their request. Anything they desired would be granted to them. Of course, it is certainly within the realms of God's Word. God will never contradict his word. There are misinterpretations of these scriptures by those who lust for things and would ask for something outside of God's will. The other extreme misinterpretation is that we should not ask for things that we desire. It contradicts God's will. God delights in giving us His heart's desire.

John 15: 7 If you remain in Me, and My words remain in you, you will ask whatever you desire, and it shall be done for you.

John 16: 24 Until now you have asked nothing in My name. Ask, and you will receive, that your joy may be full.

Luke 12: 31 But seek the kingdom of God, and all these things shall be given to you.

32 "Do not be afraid, little flock, for it is your Father's good pleasure to give you the kingdom.

Many Christians do not realize that God receives much joy as we pray believing for something knowing that God is good. God delights in giving us our heart's desires. God enjoys giving to us. Just as you may delight in giving the best to your loved ones, God delights in giving to us. So many people do not know how good God is. I am talking about Christians. They live beneath their privileges in God. They believe the lie that is not spiritual to pray believing for something you desire. As long it is not contrary to God's Word, God delights in answering our prayers.

The blessings are of covenant

Many Christians do not know the blessings of God's covenant with Moses. God promised to bless his people in all areas of their lives, spiritual and financial and every other way. Jesus fulfilled the laws given to Moses by God. Because of our faith in Jesus Christ, we inherit the promises of God to His people.

Galatians 3: 14 so that the blessing of Abraham might come on the Gentiles through Jesus Christ, that we might receive the promise of the Spirit through faith.

Galatians 3: 16 Now the promises were made to Abraham and his Seed. He does not say, "and to seeds," meaning many, but "and to your Seed,"[g] meaning one, who is Christ. 17 And this I say, that the law, which came four hundred and thirty years later, does not annul the covenant that was ratified by God in Christ, so as to nullify the promise. 18 For if the inheritance comes from the law, it no longer comes from the promise. But God gave it to Abraham through a promise.

God promised Moses the blessings listed in the book of Deuteronomy. Part of the blessing included keeping God's Word and living Holy. Part of it included God blessing people so they would be overflowing with prosperity, children, crops, animals and blessings upon the land to be rich and fertile. The promises include special favour and treasure from God both spiritual and earthly. Certainly, part of the blessing is that the people would obey the commandments of God all the days of their lives.

Deuteronomy 28: 9 The Lord will establish you as a holy people to Himself, just as He swore to you, if you will keep the commandments of the Lord your God and walk in His ways. 10 All people of the earth shall see that you are called by the name of the Lord, and they shall be afraid of you. 11 The Lord will make you overflow in prosperity, in the offspring of your body, in the offspring of your livestock, and in the produce of your ground, in the land which the Lord swore to your fathers to give you.

12 The Lord will open up to you His good treasure, the heavens, to give the rain to your land in its season and to bless all the work of your hand. You will lend to many nations, but you will not borrow. 13 The Lord will make you the head and not the tail; you will only be above and you will not be beneath, if you listen to the commandments of the Lord your God, which I am commanding you today, to observe and to do them. 14 Also, you shall

not turn aside from any of the words which I am commanding you today, to the right hand or to the left, to go after other gods to serve them.

Chapter 6
End of chapter questions

1. Explain uour prayer life in terms of how you pray. There should be worship, prayer for yourself and prayer for people and things God places on your heart.
2. If you do not usually pray for the government of your region, start praying for the government officials as it is a commandment that God gave us.
3. If there was an instance in your life that you believe God spoke to you in some way before you became a Christian, explain it and how you know it was God.

7 LIVING BY FAITH

Chapter 7

We Christians have the indwelling presence of God constantly; it gives us confidence in God knowing that He hears us and answers our prayers.

Living by faith means literally believing God's Word and living it. The Word of God is the final authority concerning all matters of human life. Living by faith is not living by the trends of the day or the system of the culture's ideas of right and wrong. It means our lives align with God's Word. Faith in God's Word gives us boldness because we know God's Word is his will. God's ways are given to us in His word.

The more Word of God we receive, pray, praise, confess and live, gives us more boldness in our prayers. I would explain it as this, if you knew most certainly your mum had made a pie for the family and she would gladly give you a piece or more, you would have boldness about getting a piece. You would have the confidence that you were included in the blessings. The same is true in the spirit. You most certainly would have boldness asking for a promise of God knowing that God's promises are His will concerning believers.

1 John 5: 14 This is the confidence that we have in Him, that if we ask anything according to His will, He hears us. 15 So if we know that He hears whatever we ask, we know that we have whatever we asked of Him.

Faith – manifests the thing we are believing from in the spirit. We believe for it and it becomes spiritual substance. We should praise God for it even before we see it manifest in the physical realm. Faith is essential for receiving from God.

Hebrews 11: 1 Now faith is the substance of things hoped for, the evidence of things not seen. 2 For by it the men of old obtained a good report.

3 By faith we understand that the universe was framed by the word of God, so that things that are seen were not made out of things which are visible.

Abraham

Abraham had faith in God even though he never saw him. He knew it was God speaking to him and he obeyed. His obedience lead to the nation of Israel. God made promises to him and kept them. God honours that covenant that he made with Abraham today though the nation of Israel and all Jewish people. If you do not believe that God is, you can receive from God. If you do not know that God is a rewarder of those who diligently seek him, you will not expect God to bless you and you will not receive the same measure of blessing of a believer living by faith in God`s Word. God will bless you, but you will be living below your privileges. It would be as though I gave you a gift card with a $100 credit. If you went shopping and bought something for 15 dollars, that would be what you obtained. Someone who used the card to purchase $100. Worth of stuff would be using his privilege fully.

FAITH

Hebrews 11: 6 And without faith it is impossible to please God, for he who comes to God must believe that He exists and that He is a rewarder of those who diligently seek Him.

By faith Abraham received from God repeatedly throughout his life. It is amazing because he did not have the indwelling presence of God, nor the written word of God. He had the promises of God and he believed. By faith both he and Sarah received and even though they were close to 100 years old, Sarah gave birth to a child whose life directly lead to the 12 tribes of Israel and the mighty nation of Israel.

Hebrews 11: 8 By faith Abraham obeyed when he was called to go out into a place which he would later receive as an inheritance. He went out not knowing where he was going. 9 By faith he dwelt in the promised land, as in a foreign land, dwelling in tents with Isaac and Jacob, the heirs of the same promise, 10 for he was looking for a city which has foundations, whose builder and maker is God. 11 By faith Sarah herself also received the ability to conceive seed, and she bore a child when she was past the age, because she judged Him faithful who had promised. 12 Therefore from one man, who was as good as dead, sprang so many, a multitude as the stars of the sky and innumerable as the sand by the seashore.

Abraham

God spoke to Him. He believed. He had God`s promises and periodic visitations of God or angels. He mostly lived his life believing in those promises, living by faith. God`s promises to Abraham were not for him alone but for all of the relatives that would be birthed because of him. It includes all of Israel. By faith in Jesus Christ, it includes me and you.

Genesis 12: 1Now the Lord said to Abram, "Go from your country, your family, and your father's house to the land that I will show you.

2 I will make of you a great nation;
   I will bless you
and make your name great,
   so that you will be a blessing.
3 I will bless them who bless you
   and curse him who curses you,[a]
and in you all families of the earth
   will be blessed."

Moses lived by faith. Although he could have lived a life of luxury and ease in Egypt as a prince, he chose to side with Israel although they were slaves. Moses saved an Israelite slave that was being beaten by an Egyptian by killing the Egyptian. Because of it, he had to leave Egypt. Moses made a life in Midian and lived as a shepherd for the next forty years.

Moses – Hebrews 11: 24 By faith Moses, when he became of age, refused to be called the son of Pharaoh's daughter, 25 choosing rather to suffer affliction with the people of God than to enjoy the pleasures of sin for a time. 26 He esteemed the reproach of Christ as greater riches than the treasures in Egypt, for he looked to the reward. 27 By faith he forsook Egypt, not fearing the wrath of the king. He endured by looking to Him who is invisible. 28 By faith he kept the Passover and the sprinkling of blood, lest the one who destroys the firstborn touch them.

29 By faith they passed through the Red Sea as on dry land, which the Egyptians attempted to do, but were drowned.

While Moses was going about ordinary shepherd duties, he was a bush on the mountain. He knew it was burning but it did not burn out. He climbed the mountain, not knowing what would be there. God used the bush to get Moses to climb the mountain to speak to him. After wards Moses would go to Mount Sinai to talk directly with God.

God spoke to Moses – Exodus 3: 1 Now Moses kept the flock of Jethro his father-in-law, the priest of Midian, and he led the flock to the far side of the desert and came to the mountain of God, to Horeb. 2 The angel of the Lord appeared to him in a flame of fire from the midst of a bush, and he looked, and the bush burned with fire, but the bush was not consumed. 3 So Moses said, "I will now turn aside and see this great sight, why the bush is not burnt."

4 When the Lord saw that he turned aside to see, God called to him from out of the midst of the bush and said, "Moses, Moses."

And he said, "Here am I."

5 He said, "Do not approach here. Remove your sandals from off your feet, for the place on which you are standing is holy ground." 6 Moreover He said, "I am the God of your father, the God of Abraham, the God of Isaac, and the God of Jacob." And Moses hid his face, for he was afraid to look upon God.

7 The Lord said, "I have surely seen the affliction of My people who are in Egypt and have heard their cry on account of their taskmasters, for I know their sorrows. 8 Therefore, I have come down to deliver them out of the hand of the Egyptians, and to bring them up out of that land to a good and spacious land, to a land flowing with milk and honey, to the place of the Canaanites, the Hittites, the Amorites, the Perizzites, the Hivites, and the Jebusites. 9 Now therefore, the cry of the children of Israel has come to Me. Moreover, I have also seen the oppression with which the Egyptians are oppressing them. 10 Come now therefore, and I will send you to Pharaoh so that you may bring forth My people, the children of Israel, out of Egypt."

11 Moses said to God, "Who am I that I should go to Pharaoh and that I should bring forth the children of Israel out of Egypt?"

12 And He said, "Certainly I will be with you, and this will be a sign to you, that I have sent you: When you have brought forth the people out of Egypt, all of you shall serve God on this mountain."

13 Moses said to God, "I am going to the children of Israel and will say to them, 'The God of your fathers has sent me to you.' When they say to me, 'What is His name?' what shall I say to them?"

14 And God said to Moses, "I AM WHO I AM,"[a] and He said, "You will say this to the children of Israel, 'I AM has sent me to you.' "

15 God, moreover, said to Moses, "Thus you will say to the children of Israel, 'The Lord, the God of your fathers, the God of Abraham, the God of Isaac, and the God of Jacob, has sent me to you. This is My name forever, and this is My memorial to all generations.'

16 "Go, and gather the elders of Israel together, and say to them, 'The Lord, the God of your fathers, the God of Abraham, of Isaac, and of Jacob, appeared to me, saying, "I am indeed concerned about you and what has been done to you in Egypt. 17 Therefore, I said, I will bring you up out of the affliction of Egypt to the land of the Canaanites, the Hittites, the Amorites, the Perizzites, the Hivites, and the Jebusites, to a land flowing with milk and honey."'

Moses faith

God spoke with Moses on many occasions. God's special mercy was on Moses. God spoke with him as with a friend. The relationship with God was as a friendship with God using Moses to free Israel from slavery but also by teaching Moses to believe that whatever God said would always come to pass. Moses believed God and obeyed God. Because of Moses faith, the nation of Israel was delivered from Egypt. Because of the faith of Moses, the scriptures were given to us. Because of the faith of Moses, the nation of Israel was lead to the promised land. Because of the faith of Moses, we have the Levitical laws and commandments of God. Moses faith continues to completely affect all believers both Jew and Gentile.

God spoke to Moses as an intimate friend. The glory of God's presence was over Israel throughout the wilderness. Moses was physically glowing with the radiant glory of God. The glory of God was over Israel protecting her all throughout the wilderness.

Exodus 33: 9 And whenever Moses entered the tent, the pillar of cloud descended and stood at the entrance of the tent, and the Lord spoke with Moses. 10 When all the people saw the pillar of cloud standing at the entrance of the tent, all the people rose up and worshipped, every man at the entrance of his tent. 11 The Lord spoke to Moses face to face, just as a man speaks to his friend. When he returned to the camp, his servant Joshua, the son of Nun, a young man, did not depart from the tent.

Although certainly Moses knew God's voice and character, the glory of God would come so strong on him it changed his countenance. Moses got to speak to God in the holy presence of the almighty God. No other person had the same privilege. The glory of God was evident on Moses.

Exodus 34: 29 When Moses came down from Mount Sinai with the two tablets of testimony in the hands of Moses, when he came down from the mountain, Moses did not know that the skin of his face shone while he talked with Him. 30 So when Aaron and all the children of Israel saw Moses, amazingly, the skin of his face shone, and they were afraid to come near him. 31 But Moses called to them, and Aaron and all the rulers of the congregation returned to him, and Moses spoke to them. 32 Afterward all the children of Israel drew near, and he commanded them all that the Lord had spoken to him on Mount Sinai.

33 When Moses finished speaking with them, he put a veil over his face. 34 But whenever Moses went in before the Lord to speak with Him, he took the veil off until he came out. Then he came out and spoke to the children of Israel what he had been commanded. 35 The children of Israel saw the face of Moses, that the skin of Moses' face shone, and then Moses put the veil over his face again until he went in to speak with Him.

Moses interceded for Israel

Moses became a friend of God. Rather than simply receiving from God, he cared about God's reputation and God's vision of creating the nation of Israel. There were occasions that God was angry at the sins of Israel and would have destroyed all the people because of it. In these instances, Moses pleaded with God so that Israel might be saved. Moses reminded God of what he had promised Israel. Moses cared for the Israelites with God's heart. Because Moses had lead them from Egypt through the wilderness and saw the provision of God and the mercy of God shown to Israel all those years, Moses also loves Israel and grasps the promise that was made to Abraham was being fulfilled. Moses would pray mercy for the Israelites until God would speak words of blessing about Israel.

Exodus 32: 11 But Moses sought the favor of the Lord his God, and said, "Lord, why does Your wrath burn against Your people, whom You have brought forth from the land of Egypt with great power and with a mighty hand? 12 Why should the Egyptians speak, saying, 'With evil intent He brought them out, to kill them in the mountains and to destroy them from the face of the earth'? Turn from Your fierce wrath and relent of this harm against Your people. 13 Remember Abraham, Isaac, and Israel, Your servants, to whom You swore by Yourself, and said to them, 'I will multiply your descendants as the stars of the heavens, and all this land that I have spoken of will I give to your descendants, and they will inherit it forever.' " 14 Then the Lord relented of the harm which He said He would do to His people.

Moses and Aaron prayed for Israel

On several occasions, Israel's sins made God angry so that he would destroy them. As the people turned against Moses and blamed him for bringing them out of Egypt to die in the wilderness, and blasphemed God by not honouring God or his commandments, Moses and Aron – were God's intercessors – with words and actions praying for Israel At one point, they literally walked between people with their censors and praying for mercy so that the people would live rather than die. They had the true role of intercessor. They cared for Israel; they cared for God and were praying mercy on Israel. Although many people died for their sin, if Moses and Aaron had not interceded, it would have been many more.

You will know that you truly share God's heart for people, when you pray mercy toward them rather than judgement. You will view the people as God's people and pray for them that they would turn to God with all their being.

Leviticus 19

Moses was entrusted with the commandments and Levitical laws of God; he was also entrusted to teach the people and to establish the tabernacle of worship and the Levitical priesthood so that people could worship God and learn to serve and honour God.

God gave the scriptures to Moses so that Moses might give them to Israel. God's plan was to prosper Israel and make an everlasting covenant with His people.

Numbers 16: 46 Moses said to Aaron, "Take a censer and put fire in it from off the altar, and put in incense, and go quickly to the assembly, and make an atonement for them, because wrath has gone out from the Lord. The plague has begun." 47 Aaron took it as Moses commanded and ran into the midst of the assembly, where the plague had begun among the people. He put in incense and made an atonement for the people. 48 He stood between the dead and the living, and the plague was stopped. 49 Now those who died in the plague were fourteen thousand seven hundred, besides those that died concerning the thing of Korah. 50 Aaron returned to Moses, to the door of the tent of meeting, and the plague was stopped.

The High Life

God Spoke to Jeremiah

God called Jerimiah to be a prophet to the nation of Israel while he was still young. God assured him that he was chosen and called. God used him to speak warnings to Israel and judgements if the people did not obey. God used him to speak to the king of Israel. At first the king was completely hard hearted and rejected him. Jeremiah was imprisoned for his prophesying of judgement coming to Israel. Even though towards the end of his reign as king of Israel, he finally believes Jeremiah's prophesies but is still too hard hearted to change. Jeremiah did not get much reception or reputation by the people of Israel. Because of the words of judgement of Israel, Jeremiah was hated but God used him to warn the people and some believed him and honoured God. Truly the judgement he prophesied about came to pass as the king of Babylon invaded Israel.

Jeremiah 1: 4 Now the word of the Lord came to me, saying,

5 "Before I formed you in the womb I knew you;
and before you were born I sanctified you,
and I ordained you a prophet to the nations."

6 Then I said, "Ah, Lord God! Truly, I cannot speak, for I am a youth."

7 But the Lord said to me, "Do not say, 'I am a youth.' For you shall go everywhere that I send you, and whatever I command you, you shall speak. 8 Do not be afraid of their faces. For I am with you to deliver you," says the Lord.

9 Then the Lord put forth His hand and touched my mouth. And the Lord said to me, "Now, I have put My words in your mouth. 10 See, I have this day set you over the nations and over the kingdoms, to root out and to pull down, to destroy and to throw down, to build and to plant."

God spoke to John the Baptist

God spoke to John the Baptist and anointed him to be a prophet during Jesus life. John the Baptist preached a strong message of repentance and turning of their lives to God. He fulfilled the promise of Isaiah. He was born into a Levitical family but lived in the desert and had many people come to him to repent and seek God.

John the Baptist   Luke 3: 2 Annas and Caiaphas being the high priests, the word of God came to John the son of Zechariah in the wilderness. 3 He came into the region surrounding the Jordan, preaching the baptism of repentance for the remission of sins. 4 As it is written in the book of the words of Isaiah the prophet, saying:

"The voice of one crying in the wilderness:
'Prepare the way of the Lord;
   make His paths straight.
5 Every valley shall be filled
   and every mountain and hill shall be brought low;
and the crooked shall be made straight
   and the rough ways shall be made smooth;
6 and all flesh shall see the salvation of God.' "[a]

John the Baptist preached the coming of the Messiah. He also prophetically spoke that Jesus was the Messiah. He acknowledged that Jesus was the Messiah. Many of his disciples began to follow Jesus. John the Baptist had a short but effective ministry of pointing the people to the Messiah. Also, he knew of a certainty that Jesus was the Messiah. He prophetically lead the way so that believers in God would accept Jesus as Messiah.

John 1: 29 The next day John saw Jesus coming toward him and said, "Look, the Lamb of God, who takes away the sin of the world. 30 This is He of whom I said, 'After me comes a Man who is preferred before me, for He was before me.' 31 I did not know Him, but for this reason I came baptizing with water: so that He might be revealed to Israel."

32 Then John bore witness, saying, "I saw the Spirit descending from heaven like a dove, and it remained on Him. 33 I did not know Him, but He who sent me to baptize with water said to me, 'The One on whom you see the Spirit descending and remaining, this is He who baptizes with the Holy Spirit.' 34 I have seen and have borne witness that He is the Son of God."

Chapter 7
End of chapter questions

1. By reading about the people God spoke to in this chapter that changed Israel, describe which character you most identify with.
2. Pray for the unseen things God does for you. Thank God for the angels that surround you and people who pray for you and those who do daily service to your life.
3. Describe an occasion where you prayed for God's mercy for someone even though the person had sinned.

PROPHETIC PRAYER AND DECLARATION

Chapter 8

Jesus lived his life by faith calling those things that be not as though they were, and they manifested as he spoke them. Although Jesus was fully God and fully man, he did not use all his spiritual power as God while he was on the earth. He used faith by speaking things into existence. He used his authority to teach, preach, heal and deliver. He humbled himself as a man means although at any moment of his life he could have commanded ranks of angels or spoken judgement or could have intervened in the earth with divine power, he limited himself to the gifts of the Holy Spirit flowing through himself as a man. He lived by faith in God's Word and used the word of God as the basis for all his dealings with people so that he was the living Word of God in our midst.

Philippians 2: 5 Let this mind be in you all, which was also in Christ Jesus,
  6 who, being in the form of God,
    did not consider equality with God something to be grasped.
7 But He emptied Himself,
    taking upon Himself the form of a servant,
    and was made in the likeness of men.
8 And being found in the form of a man,
    He humbled Himself
    and became obedient to death,
      even death on a cross.
9 Therefore God highly exalted Him
    and gave Him the name which is above every name,

The Word of God with faith produces miracles.

The Word of God + faith releases explosions of glory – miracles, answers to prayer, order, solutions. Jesus spoke with authority the Word of God. After he spoke, often people were healed or delivered from demons. Miracles occurred because Jesus spoke with authority. Jesus spoke by faith and things manifested in the natural.

Romans 10: 17 So then faith comes by hearing, and hearing by the word of God.

Hebrews 4: 2 For the gospel was preached to us as well as to them. But the word preached did not benefit them, because it was not mixed with faith in those who heard it.

Jesus spoke peace – storm stopped.

As Jesus and his disciples sailed on a boat in the sea, there was a terrible storm; Jesus seemed nonchalant about it so relaxed that the disciples accused him of not caring. Jesus spoke and rebuked the storm. The storm obeyed. Jesus spoke, and the sky was calm, and the waters were calm. He spoke by faith and it impacted the weather conditions of his region. Jesus questioned the disciples on their faith. I don't believe he did it to brag but rather to stir them into using their faith in such instances to rebuke storms and command the situations. The disciples marvelled at his ability to command the storms. Jesus used the situation to teach them to use faith. Speaking with authority brings about miracles.

Mark 4: 35 That same day, when the evening came, He said to them, "Let us go cross to the other side." 36 When they had sent the crowd away, they took Him in the boat just as He was. There were also other little boats with Him. 37 A great wind storm arose, and the waves splashed into the boat, so that it was now filling the boat. 38 He was in the stern asleep on a pillow. They woke Him and said, "Teacher, do You not care that we are perishing?"

39 He rose and rebuked the wind, and said to the sea, "Peace, be still!" Then the wind ceased and there was a great calm.

40 He said to them, "Why are you so fearful? How is that you have no faith?"

41 They feared greatly and said to one another, "What kind of Man is He, that even the wind and the sea obey Him?"

Victory over death

Jesus spoke, and the dead were raised to life. On several occasions, Jesus was brought to people who had died. He raised them back to life. In the instance of his personal friend, Lazarus, Lazarus had been dead for more than 3 days. His natural body was decomposing. Jesus commanded him to return to his body and also made him completely healthy. Jesus used his faith to command resurrection life. The miracles of resurrection life are not only to build our faith but to show us that God who spoke all things into existence has power over death. Because Jesus is life, he could command the resurrection of the dead.

John 11: 40 Jesus said to her, "Did I not tell you that if you believed, you would see the glory of God?" 41 So they took away the stone from the place where the dead man was lying. Jesus lifted up His eyes and said, "Father, I thank You that You have heard Me. 42 I know that You always hear Me. But because of the people standing around, I said this, that they may believe that You sent Me."

43 When He had said this, He cried out with a loud voice, "Lazarus, come out!" 44 He who was dead came out, his hands and feet wrapped with grave clothes, and his face wrapped with a cloth.

Jesus said to them, "Unbind him, and let him go."

Later the resurrection of the dead occurs with the Apostle Peter and the Apostle Paul. They were speaking by faith in the living Christ.

Acts 9: 39 Peter rose up and went with them. When he arrived, they led him into the upper room. All the widows stood by him weeping and showing the tunics and garments which Dorcas had made while she was with them.

40 Peter put them all outside and knelt down and prayed. And turning to the body he said, "Tabitha, arise." She opened her eyes, and when she saw Peter she sat up. 41 He gave her his hand and lifted her up. And when he had called the saints and widows, he presented her alive. 42 It became known throughout all Joppa, and many believed in the Lord.

The Apostle Paul raised Eutychus from the dead.

Acts 20: 9 A young man named Eutychus sat in the window, falling into a deep sleep as Paul spoke for a longer time. Being overcome by sleep, he fell down from the third floor and was taken up dead. 10 Paul went down and leaned over him, and embracing him said, "Do not be troubled, for he is alive." 11 When he had gone up and had broken bread and eaten, he conversed for a long while until dawn and departed.

 The word of God that Jesus is life and life everlasting mixed with faith speaks resurrection life over people. It can be spiritual. It can be physical. There are modern day testimonies of people who have been raised from the dead. Jesus is the resurrection and the life because He is life – the essence of life.

John 11: 25 Jesus said to her, "I am the resurrection and the life. He who believes in Me, though he may die, yet shall he live. 26 And whoever lives and believes in Me shall never die. Do you believe this?"

Jesus spoke healing

There are many instances of Jesus bringing healing to people throughout the scriptures. He spoke words of faith that brought results. He had the authority over all sickness because He is life. He spoke forgiveness of sins, because he would die to redeem us from sin. Jesus words were faith words. He not only forgave the sins of the person, but he also brought healing to them.

Jesus spoke and forgave sins and brought healing

Matthew 9: 1 He entered a boat, crossed over, and came into His own city. 2 They brought to Him a man sick with paralysis, lying on a bed. And Jesus, seeing their faith, said to the paralytic, "Son, be of good cheer. Your sins are forgiven you."

3 Then certain scribes said within themselves, "This Man blasphemes."

4 Jesus, knowing their thoughts, said, "Why do you think evil in your hearts? 5 For which is easier, to say, 'Your sins are forgiven you' or to say, 'Arise and walk'? 6 But that you may know that the Son of Man has authority on earth to forgive sins"—then He said to the paralytic, "Arise, pick up your bed, and go into your house." 7 And he rose and departed to his house. 8 But when the crowds saw it, they were amazed and glorified God who had given such authority to men.

Mark 2: 2 Immediately many were gathered together, so that there was no room to receive them, not even at the door. And He preached the word to them. 3 They came to Him bringing one sick with paralysis, who was carried by four men. 4 When they could not come near Him due to the crowding, they uncovered the roof where He was. When they had broken it open, they let down the bed on which the paralytic lay. 5 When Jesus saw their faith, He said to the paralytic, "Son, your sins are forgiven you."

6 But some of the scribes were sitting there, reasoning in their hearts, 7 "Why does this Man speak such blasphemies? Who can forgive sins but God alone?"

8 Immediately, when Jesus perceived in His spirit that they so reasoned within themselves, He said to them, "Why do you contemplate these things in your hearts? 9 Which is easier to say to the paralytic: 'Your sins are

forgiven you,' or to say, 'Rise, take up your bed and walk'? 10 But that you may know that the Son of Man has authority on earth to forgive sins," He said to the paralytic, 11 "I say to you, rise, and take up your bed, and go your way to your house." 12 Immediately he rose, picked up the bed, and went out in front of them all, so that they were all amazed and glorified God, saying, "We never saw anything like this!"

Jesus strength and way of building his faith was to withdraw and pray alone. He often did this after a miracle or after a healing. He was renewing his faith with God and he was avoiding the temptation to succumb to the people who wanted to make him the king. He resisted the temptation and strengthened himself with his relationship with God.

Jesus prayed often – going off alone to pray or seek God. In this instance Jesus saw their hearts would have made him a king. He escaped their plans by withdrawing.

John 6: 14 When those men saw the sign which He had done, they then said, "This is truly the Prophet who is to come into the world." 15 Therefore, knowing that they would come and take Him by force to make Him king, Jesus departed again to a mountain by Himself alone.

In this instance Jesus withdraws because he not only saw the people but could discern their hearts and motives. He knew his mission and stayed true to it and was not distracted by the promise of fame or earthly wealth.

John 2: 23 Now when He was in Jerusalem at the Passover Feast, many believed in His name when they saw the signs which He did. 24 But Jesus did not entrust Himself to them, because He knew all men, 25 and did not need anyone to bear witness of man, for He knew what was in man.

Matthew 12: 15 But when Jesus knew it, He withdrew from there. And great crowds followed Him, and He healed them all, 16 and warned them that they should not make Him known, 17 to fulfill what was spoken by Isaiah the prophet, saying:
18 "Here is My Servant, whom I have chosen,

My Beloved, in whom My soul is well pleased;
I will put My Spirit upon Him,
   and He will render judgment to the Gentiles.
19 He shall not struggle nor cry out,
   nor will anyone hear His voice in the streets.
20 A bruised reed He will not break,

and a smoldering wick He will not quench,
until He renders judgment unto victory;
21   and in His name will the Gentiles trust."[a]

Luke 5: 15 Yet even more so His fame went everywhere. And great crowds came together to hear and to be healed by Him of their infirmities. 16 But He withdrew to the wilderness and prayed.

If Jesus, the son of God, the Messiah had to withdraw to pray and encourage himself in the things of God, how important that we also keep all things in light of eternity. We must be speaking with the Holy Spirit and obey His promptings, to complete our main purpose for life not being distracted by promises of fame or wealth. Please see fame in itself is not wrong. If God has given you fame – stay humble; acknowledge God and keep to your mission. If God has given you earthly wealth, use it for his glory. Jesus knew his mission was to come die for all people so that we might be saved, restored to God. Jesus kept his mission as the main aspect of his life.

It is essential to know your purpose and to keep it. People who know their purpose in life, are often connected to the right people, to specific regions of the earth, and to their gifts and callings. God will prosper you in your area of authority. It is essential that you know your giftings and callings and the purpose God has for your life. I only mention it here but teach on it in detail in both my books Living Life Fully and in Living the High Calling. I recommend them to you if you do not know your purpose or what you should be doing on the earth.

Jesus Prayed

If Jesus knew it had to draw away from the crowds to pray and be refreshed by God's presence – certainly we also should do the same. Although he did miracles, signs and wonders, Jesus knew the source of his strength and often withdrew to go pray. We should do whatever is necessary to build up ourselves spiritually in faith.

Jude 1: 20 But you, beloved, build yourselves up in your most holy faith. Pray in the Holy Spirit. 21 Keep yourselves in the love of God while you are waiting for the mercy of our Lord Jesus Christ, which leads to eternal life.

Faith prays to get connect with God. Faith receives the answer before it manifests in the natural realm. Faith speaks and things that do not exist come into existence to align with words of faith.

Romans 4: 16 Therefore the promise comes through faith, so that it might be by grace, that the promise would be certain to all the descendants, not only to those who are of the law, but also to those who are of the faith of Abraham, who is the father of us all 17 (as it is written, "I have made you a father of many nations"[c]) before God whom he believed, and who raises the dead, and calls those things that do not exist as though they did.

It is important to build up your own faith and to boost your own faith with scriptures and spiritual songs and by stirring up your giftings. Immersing yourself in worship and praise, preaching and teaching, scripture and psalms and spiritual songs is a way of feeding your spirit man so you can be strengthened and renewed in faith.

Ephesians 5: 19 Speak to one another in psalms, hymns, and spiritual songs, singing and making melody in your heart to the Lord. 20 Give thanks always for all things to God the Father in the name of our Lord Jesus Christ, 21 being submissive to one another in the fear of God.

2 Timothy 1: 6 Therefore I remind you to stir up the gift of God, which is in you by the laying on of my hands.

Words spoken with faith – reveal the issues of the heart – impact the life around us.

Just as a mighty force can be used for good – it can also be used negatively. It is necessary to guard your mouth; it is necessary to align your words with God's words.

Psalm 19: 14 Let the words of my mouth and the meditation of my heart
be acceptable in Your sight,
O Lord, my strength and my Redeemer.

Matthew 12:35 A good man out of the good treasure of his heart brings forth good things. And an evil man out of the evil treasure brings forth evil things. 36 But I say to you that for every idle word that men speak, they will give an account on the Day of Judgment. 37 For by your words you will be justified, and by your words you will be condemned."

The importance of words cannot be overstated. Once you realize the words you speak affect those around you and can make a difference encouraging, exhorting or comforting or instructing people, you will desire to speak in alignment with God's Word and not speak negative or foolish words.

Chapter 8
End of chapter questions

1. Considering that words directly affect your life, pray asking the Holy Spirit to help you choose words wisely and if you don't that the Holy Spirit would correct you.
2. When you pray, believe. If necessary, stir your faith before, during and after your prayers. Pray in faith believing and receiving in the spirit from God.
3. Describe an occasion where you spoke the word of God by faith and brought peace to a situation. If this has not occurred, pray that God would use you to be a peacemaker.

9 THE ENGRAFTED WORD

Chapter 9
The engrafted word – becoming one with God's Word

Because Jesus is the Living Word of God, He and God's Word are one. Christians read God's word, pray God's Word and confess God's Word. What occurs is that the word of God becomes so rooted in our spirits that it becomes engrafted to our very souls. We become living epistles. The Word of God becomes inseparable from our own spirit. We align with the Word of God until we live the word of God consistently.

James 1: 21 Therefore lay aside all filthiness and remaining wickedness and receive with meekness the engrafted word, which is able to save your souls.

Romans 12: 12 I urge you therefore, brothers, by the mercies of God, that you present your bodies as a living sacrifice, holy, and acceptable to God, which is your reasonable service of worship. 2 Do not be conformed to this world, but be transformed by the renewing of your mind, that you may prove what is the good and acceptable and perfect will of God.

God's word is important for prayer to align with God's Word. It is so much more important to digest it until it becomes a nutrient to us – one with us. Only by reading God's Word, hearing God's word, praying and confessing God's Word can we get it into the spirit. God's Word becomes the centre of our identity – we identify with God's Word. It is not always apparent to us as we are being transformed from glory to glory. Others may see it in us. We will desire to do the will of God and it will be expressed in good works that glorify God. We will give; we will serve; we will encourage; we will show mercy. We will care for the poor, the widow, the orphan and identify with others with compassion and action though we may never meet them. We will care about all the people on earth not only our family or church. The Word of God completely transforms our character.

It doesn't mean that we stop existing in our identity. It rather causes us as individuals to magnify God with the Spirit of God shining through us. God frees us to live as we choose. Once a Christian realizes the best possible life is living with God and living by the scriptures, he or she shines the light of Christ through his or her human spirit and soul.

Aligning your life with the Word

It is essential that Christians know how to choose scriptures that build up, encourage and feed their spirit man. The only way of doing this is to dig in the Word of God. It involves searching scriptures that agree on certain topics and applying them to our lives by prayer and study. Repetition of the scripture to various aspects of our lives is necessary. One scripture can impact our lives in various ways. It means the Word of God is truth in your life. You are living the Word.

Finding a scripture in the Scriptures (Logos) that is applicable to your life. Get several scriptures – write them. Pray them. Confess them. Pray in agreement with what God says about your situation.

God's Word never returns void.

Isaiah 55: 8 For My thoughts are not your thoughts,
nor are your ways My ways,
says the Lord.
9 For as the heavens are higher than the earth,
so are My ways higher than your ways,
and My thoughts than your thoughts.
10 For as the rain comes down,
and the snow from heaven,
and do not return there
but water the earth
and make it bring forth and bud
that it may give seed to the sower and bread to the eater,
11 so shall My word be that goes forth from My mouth;
it shall not return to Me void,
but it shall accomplish that which I please,
and it shall prosper in the thing for which I sent it.

God's word never returns void means that the word of God is always effective. It is potent. I am a gardener and have sown seeds to grow both flowers and vegetables. I carefully place the seeds, but I always plant more seeds than I need because some seeds are dormant or do not sprout. There may also be birds and other creatures that dig up those seeds. The point is the seeds sprout. God word always sprouts unlike the natural seeds. God's word always produces after its kind.
As a radish seed always produces radishes, God's Word produces after itself.

For instance, the word of God following can be applied to many areas of our human life:

2 Corinthians 2: 14 Now thanks be to God who always causes us to triumph in Christ and through us reveals the fragrance of His knowledge in every place.

The scripture of God causing us to triumph can be applied to sports. We can pray it over ourselves and believe and confess it so that we can give our best physical effort in sports. Also, in terms of finances, we can confess the word and receive the increase of finances because of the word always causes us to triumph. It can also be applied to our careers. We can claim triumph or victory to do our best in our jobs because God's Word can apply to all situations of our existence.

Should you receive a Word from God that produces fruit in one area of your life, start applying it to other areas in your life. Pray that the Holy Spirit may give you revelation or insight on how it can apply to every aspect of your life. The Holy Spirit can quicken the revelation of it to you and you will receive a harvest of increase from the scripture.

Just as a radish seed produces radishes, the word of God produces fruit. Radishes can be used in salads or in snacks or as a decoration etc. The Word of God can be applied in many areas also.

God's word is eternal. Although heaven and earth and all that we know of our solar system will one day pass away, God's word never will. God's Word is eternal.

1 Peter 1: 22 Since your souls have been purified by obedience to the truth through the Spirit unto a genuine brotherly love, love one another deeply with a pure heart, 23 for you have been born again, not from perishable seed, but imperishable, through the word of God which lives and abides forever. 24 For
"All flesh is as grass,
 and all the glory of man as the flower of grass.
The grass withers, and its flower falls away,
25   but the word of the Lord endures forever."[b]

Digest the Word

The best way to get the word of God into you is to attend a Bible study. Church sermons usually build you up and encourage you. If they do not, I would recommend a church where God's word is preached with faith. Reading your Bible regularly and praying the scriptures are other ways of ingesting the Word. Confessing the word in your life situations also gets it into your spirit. What occurs often is revelation of how God's word applies to your life. It is the revelation of the Word that is the RHEMA word of God. It is the Holy Spirit Himself quickening that word to you. They are not different completely. Just as a parent gives a baby his or her food, we feed our spirit on purpose, receiving God's Word. If we give ourselves to feeding on the word of God daily, there will be revelations and inspirations of the Holy Spirit. God Himself will speak clearly to us through the Word.

This is the word that was preached to you.

Prophetic word of God – God speaks and so it is.

Isaiah 40: 3 The voice of him who cries out,
"Prepare the way of the Lord
   in the wilderness,
make straight in the desert
   a highway for our God.
4 Let every valley be lifted up,
   and every mountain and hill be made low,
and let the rough ground become a plain,
   and the rough places a plain;
5 then the glory of the Lord shall be revealed,
   and all flesh shall see it together,
   for the mouth of the Lord has spoken it."

6 The voice said, "Cry out."
   And he said, "What shall I cry out?"

All flesh is grass,
   and all its loveliness is as the flower of the field.
7 The grass withers, the flower fades
   because the Spirit of the Lord blows upon it;
   surely the people are grass.
8 The grass withers, the flower fades,
   but the word of our God shall stand forever.

Because God and his word are inseparable, His word has creative potential. It always produces. It is always living seed that produces. God spoke by faith and created all things. He spoke light into existence. He spoke that the waters and land would be distinguished. He spoke plants and vegetation into existence. He made all creatures and all living things reproduce after their kind.

God's Word brings miracles.

Genesis 1: 3 God said, "Let there be light," and there was light. 4 God saw that the light was good, and God separated the light from the darkness. 5 God called the light Day, and the darkness He called Night. So the evening and the morning were the first day.

6 Then God said, "Let there be an expanse in the midst of the waters, and let it separate the waters from the waters." 7 So God made the expanse and separated the waters which were under the expanse from the waters which were above the expanse. And it was so. 8 God called the expanse Heaven. So the evening and the morning were the second day.

9 Then God said, "Let the waters under the heavens be gathered together into one place, and let the dry land appear." And it was so. 10 God called the dry land Earth, and the gathering together of the waters He called Seas. Then God saw that it was good.

11 Then God said, "Let the earth produce vegetation:[c] plants yielding seed and fruit trees on the earth yielding fruit after their kind with seed in them." And it was so. 12 The earth produced vegetation, plants yielding seed after their kind and trees yielding fruit with seed in them after their kind. And God saw that it was good. 13 So the evening and the morning were the third day.

14 And God said, "Let there be lights in the expanse of the heavens to separate the day from the night, and let them be signs to indicate seasons, and days, and years. 15 Let them be lights in the expanse of the heavens to give light on the earth." And it was so. 16 God made two great lights: the greater light to rule the day and the lesser light to rule the night. He made the stars also. 17 Then God set them in the expanse of the heavens to give light on the earth, 18 to rule over the day and over the night, and to divide the light from the darkness. Then God saw that it was good. 19 So the evening and the morning were the fourth day.

20 Then God said, "Let the waters swarm with swarms of living creatures and let the birds fly above the earth in the open expanse of the heavens." 21 So God created great sea creatures and every living thing that moves, with

which the waters swarmed, according to their kind, and every winged bird according to its kind. And God saw that it was good. 22 Then God blessed them, saying, "Be fruitful and multiply and fill the waters in the seas, and let the birds multiply on the earth." 23 So the evening and the morning were the fifth day.

24 Then God said, "Let the earth bring forth living creatures according to their kinds: livestock, and creeping things, and beasts of the earth according to their kinds." And it was so. 25 So God made the beasts of the earth according to their kind, and the livestock according to their kind, and everything that creeps on the earth according to its kind. And God saw that it was good.

God created man

God created all living things to reproduce but he gave man a special trait that we could have free will. In this way we are spiritual beings. We can choose to live for God or not. God gave man dominion over all creatures and over all the realms of the earth. God gave us not only privilege but responsibility. Adam named all creatures. Although they were already created, God let Adam speak their names. In this way, mankind is like God. We can speak by faith or not.

Genesis 1: 26 Then God said, "Let us make man in our image, after our likeness, and let them have dominion over the fish of the sea, and over the birds of the air, and over the livestock, and over all the earth, and over every creeping thing that creeps on the earth."

27 So God created man in His own image;
   in the image of God He created him;
   male and female He created them.

28 God blessed them and said to them, "Be fruitful and multiply, and replenish the earth and subdue it. Rule over the fish of the sea and over the birds of the air and over every living thing that moves on the earth."

29 Then God said, "See, I have given you every plant yielding seed which is on the face of all the earth and every tree which has fruit yielding seed. It shall be food for you. 30 To every beast of the earth and to every bird of the air and to everything that creeps on the earth which has the breath of life in it, I have given every green plant for food." And it was so.

31 God saw everything that He had made, and indeed it was very good. So

the evening and the morning were the sixth day.
God spoke it

God spoke it. It occurred. It was as it should be – exactly as it should be. Because He is omnipotent whatever He says will manifest. Similarly, God gave us a measure of faith. Whatever we speak in faith believing will manifest. Confessing the scriptures by faith produces godly fruit in our lives. Confessing negative words affects us. Examples are people who are always negative who are usually ill. We can speak negative things believing them and see them affect our health, our joy, our spirit. It is so essential that we sow kind words into our children's lives, into our families' lives and into those in our sphere of authority.

I am saying you Christian can affect your life by your words. Speak on purpose. Speak by faith.

Mark 11: 22 Jesus answered them, "Have faith in God. 23 For truly I say to you, whoever says to this mountain, 'Be removed and be thrown into the sea,' and does not doubt in his heart, but believes that what he says will come to pass, he will have whatever he says. 24 Therefore I say to you, whatever things you ask when you pray, believe that you will receive them, and you will have them.

Matthew 21: 21 Jesus answered them, "Truly I say to you, if you have faith and do not doubt, you will not only do what was done to the fig tree, but also, if you say to this mountain, 'Be removed, and be thrown into the sea,' it will be done. 22 And whatever you ask in prayer, if you believe, you will receive."

Belief affects life

Even secular scientists have proven that what a person says and believes about himself or herself will affect his or her life. It affects the person's thoughts, beliefs, goals, attitude etc. How much more should we as Christians not only believe, speak and pray, but also give testimony of how God's Word has produced in out lives. We should be telling others what God has done for us. Not only is it good for us, but it is a living epistle. It is God's word proven through our lives that inspires others to believe God themselves.

God's Word is spirit; God's word is life. The Word of God is unlike any other type of words. They are spiritual, and they are living. We Christians have the privilege of speaking God's words over ourselves, over our situations, over others. We become willing participants or servants of God by speaking God's Word to others.

John 6: 63 It is the Spirit who gives life. The flesh profits nothing. The words that I speak to you are spirit and are life.

2 Corinthians 3: 2 You are our letter written in our hearts, known and read by all men. 3 For you are prominently declared to be the letter of Christ, prepared by us, written not with ink but with the Spirit of the living God, not on tablets of stone but on human tablets of the heart.

God spoke to people: it changed their world

Examples of How God spoke to individuals that impacted their world are discussed throughout the scriptures. One scripture quickened by God can totally change your world. You could offer a word of hope or joy or encouragement to someone and completely change the person by sowing light.

1 Thessalonians 5: 5 You are all the sons of light and the sons of the day. We are not of the night nor of darkness.

Ephesians 5: 8 For you were formerly darkness, but now you are light in the Lord. Walk as children of light— 9 for the fruit of the Spirit is in all goodness and righteousness and truth— 10 proving what is pleasing to the Lord.

Abraham

God spoke to people throughout the scriptures. He instructed them and led them. They transformed their world. Abraham heard God and obeyed. Genesis 12, 13, 26. Because of Abraham's obedience and faith, the nation of Israel was birthed in the spirit as God imparted His blessing to Abraham that is even present thousands of years later upon all of Israel.

Moses

Moses obeyed God. Result that Israel was delivered from slavery in Egypt. It was a fulfillment of the promises God made to Abraham as well as a fulfillment of what God promised Moses. It ushered in the Covenant of God's commandments. Judaism began with God speaking to Moses and establishing the commandments.

Hebrews 11: 27 By faith he forsook Egypt, not fearing the wrath of the king. He endured by looking to Him who is invisible. 28 By faith he kept the Passover and the sprinkling of blood, lest the one who destroys the firstborn touch them.

29 By faith they passed through the Red Sea as on dry land, which the Egyptians attempted to do, but were drowned.

Elijah

God called Elijah to be a prophet over Israel. He spoke with kings. He was not liked by wicked people because he honoured God and spoke God's words. He had to run from both Ahab and Jezebel the wicked queen. He had a magnificent victory for God by his faith offering a sacrifice to God as the Baal worshippers were trying to offer a sacrifice. Afterwards, he personally slays hundreds of prophets of Baal. It is a victory that let all of those present see the glory in Jehovah as God received the offering of Elijah with mighty miracles.

Afterwards, Jezebel pledged to murder him. Elijah ran and hid in a cave. God met him there and spoke to him about his attitude. Elijah was hiding rather than living by faith. His words were negative. He believed he was the only prophet of God left because he was the only one he knew of. His confession was what he believed. God corrected him by speaking with him on that mountain.

1 Kings 19: 9 He came to a cave and camped there, and the word of the Lord came to him, and He said to him, "Why are you here, Elijah?"

10 And he said, "I have been very zealous for the Lord, Lord of Hosts, for the children of Israel have forsaken Your covenant, thrown down Your altars, and killed Your prophets with the sword, and I alone am left, and they seek to take my life."

11 He said, "Go and stand on the mountain before the Lord."

And, behold, the Lord passed by, and a great and strong wind split the mountains and broke in pieces the rocks before the Lord, but the Lord was not in the wind. And after the wind, an earthquake came, but the Lord was not in the earthquake. 12 And after the earthquake, a fire came, but the Lord was not in the fire, and after the fire, a still, small voice. 13 When Elijah heard it, he wrapped his face in his cloak and went out and stood in the entrance to the cave.

God showed evidence of his might by his use of the elements of wind, earthquake, fire. Afterwards, finally, God spoke in a quiet voice. God was showing that He truly is God. Certainly, that should have built up Elijah's faith. Knowing that God is omnipotent should build faith but only truly hearing God's Word does build faith. Miracles and mighty signs can help someone who already believes and can draw people to want to know God, but only receiving the word of God into the spirit can build faith.

Romans 10: 17 So then faith comes by hearing, and hearing by the word of God.

Once God speaks and a person receives the word with faith, the purpose is revealed. Please note that God does not speak to people or do miracles for entertainment. God always has a purpose. God was still using him as a prophet.

God spoke to him the same message, but Elijah replied the same reply. It was not a faith reply.
God corrected Elijah and instructed him to obey to anoint the new king, to anoint Hazeal to be king over Aram. He commanded him to anoint Jehu to be king over Israel and Elisha to be the new prophet who would succeed him.

And a voice came to him and said, "Why are you here, Elijah?"

1 Kings 19: 14 And he said, "I have been very zealous for the Lord, Lord of Hosts, because the children of Israel have forsaken Your covenant, thrown down Your altars, and killed your prophets with the sword, and I alone am left, and they seek to take my life."

15 The Lord said to him, "Go, return on the road through the Wilderness of Damascus, and when you arrive, anoint Hazael to be king over Aram. 16 And you shall anoint Jehu, the son of Nimshi, to be king over Israel, and you shall anoint Elisha, the son of Shaphat of Abel Meholah, to be prophet in your place. 17 He who escapes the sword of Hazael will be killed by Jehu, and he who escapes the sword of Jehu will be killed by Elisha. 18 Still, I have preserved seven thousand men in Israel for Myself, all of whose knees have not bowed to Baal and whose mouths have not kissed him."

God made it clear that his perspective was different form Elijah's. God was planning a future for Israel. God had preserved thousands of faithful believers unto himself.

These people God spoke to, changed their nation. One word of God can radically impact your life and all the people within your spheres of authority and beyond what you even know.

Chapter 9
End of chapter questions

1. God spoke all things into existence by faith. Consider the most beautiful places you have been to. Thank God for the beauty of those places. Pray that God would make you a wise steward of all within your sphere of authority.
2. Speak kind words on purpose to those in your life to encourage them – in your everyday people. Especially thank those who serve you by giving them a smile, thanksgiving and also something special such as water or a beverage.
3. Realize that the words you speak in faith directly impact the world. Remember to pray for angels to be released to bring it to come to pass.
4. Consider sowing God's word into people's lives – even one scripture a day. You could post it to social media or write a letter or an email. That word, sown prayerfully can totally affect someone's life.

CONCLUSION

Conclusion

It is my prayer that this book will encourage you in your prayer life and your faith. Most importantly that you will realize God the Holy Spirit communicates with you and desires to use you as an agent of righteousness in your spheres of authority. It will mean that you realize your life has a meaning beyond itself. You will begin to pray for God to use you and you will by faith receive assignments where God will use you to pray for someone or give or encourage or help someone. These instances are a joy to the servant of God because he or she becomes a willing servant of God helping people.

God speaks to people. Jesus speaks to us. We will recognize his voice.

John 10: 14 "I am the good shepherd. I know My sheep and am known by My own. 15 Even as the Father knows Me, so I know the Father. And I lay down My life for the sheep.

John 10: 27 My sheep hear My voice, and I know them, and they follow Me. 28 I give them eternal life. They shall never perish, nor shall anyone snatch them from My hand.

Pray that you would clearly know God's voice so that the Holy Spirit can help you throughout your day, each day.

Discerning

It is essential to know how to discern God's voice. God never contradicts His word. That means anything you receive from God (word, dream, vision, scripture) will always be in line with the scriptures. God will never speak to you, things that contradict the scriptures so, it is essential for all Christians to know God's Word: to read, to study, to pray and to live God's word.

God's Word brings peace

God's Word is inseparable from God's will. Learning the scriptures and the truths that apply to all situations of our life can only be revealed to us through the Holy Spirit who dwells within us. If you believe God has spoken to you something but do not have peace about it, pray for revelation. If necessary, fast and pray so that you can get yourself focussed on God so that he might reveal to you truth. Throughout the scriptures, God would speak things to people, but He always brought peace in the interpretation. Even Daniel who saw future things was comforted by an angel of the LORD. Never settle for less than God's best. God will always give you peace no matter what He speaks to you. If you do not feel peace, you must pray to get further revelation or insight. You should seek God because perhaps you did not understand or perhaps you must have further revelation to see it from a divine perspective.

God's Word is eternal

There is always an issue of God speaking for eternity when God speaks to us. It is not only for one situation. The rhema word or word quickened by the Holy Spirit is a revealed word that can apply throughout all our lives. As we hold onto the promises of God by faith believing, we can get revelation from the Holy Spirit who will always bring clarity and peace with it. Since the word is for all your life, you should write it in a special place, pray it and teach it to others.

2 Timothy 2: 2 Share the things that you have heard from me in the presence of many witnesses with faithful men who will be able to teach others also.

The RHEMA Word

Once God speaks something to you it is for all your life long. Should God quicken a scripture to you, keep it special and review it, pray it, pray for God to show you how to apply it.

Align with scripture – Keep God's Word as your priority

It is necessary that we live aligning with the Word of God as our priority. Literally start praising God thanking Him for His Word. Thank God for the revelation He brings to you. We hold onto the commandments and live by them through faith in Jesus Christ. God's Word always brings light or revelation. If we sin, we repent quickly so that the enemy has nothing. We esteem the scriptures as the final authority concerning our lives. We read the word, study, pray and confess it. It brings light to us.

Psalm 119: 129 Your testimonies are wonderful;
   therefore my soul keeps them.
130 The giving of Your words gives light;
   it grants understanding to the simple.

Praying the scriptures and confessing them engrafts the word into our inner soul. We are changed by God's Word.

It is important to have a Christian friend to whom you can speak with about spiritual things. You should not share the things of god with just anyone. It should be someone who truly loves you unconditionally. It should be someone who knows God and has a close relationship with Him. A true Christian friend will always value you and care for you. The person will not be self seeking but care for your best interest as well as encourage you in spiritual things. If you do not have such a friend, pray that God may bring some into your life.

Proverbs 27: 17 Iron sharpens iron,
  so a man sharpens the countenance of his friend.

If you are not certain about what God has spoken to you, get a mature friend to pray about it with you about the word of God you believe you have received. Often a spiritual friend will bring revelation to such a situation.

Pray for confirmation. One word from God can confirm something God has spoken to you. It can come through a song or a hymn or a prophecy or preaching or reading your Bible.

Keep the word

Keep the Word of God as a priority. Let the Holy Spirit quicken the word of God to you by asking Him for revelation. Treasure the Word of God. Those who do, prosper spiritually as well as in all other ways.

Joshua 1: 6 "Be strong and courageous, for you shall provide the land that I swore to their fathers to give them as an inheritance for this people. 7 Be strong and very courageous, in order to act carefully in accordance with all the law that My servant Moses commanded you. Do not turn aside from it to the right or the left, so that you may succeed wherever you go. 8 This Book of the Law must not depart from your mouth. Meditate on it day and night so that you may act carefully according to all that is written in it. For then you will make your way successful, and you will be wise. 9 Have not I commanded you? Be strong and courageous. Do not be afraid or dismayed, for the Lord your God is with you wherever you go."

Keep God's word before you in your eyes. Read it often. Keep it in your ears. Say it; pray it; receive it by faith out loud. Keep God's Word in your heart. Pray literally: God engraft this truth into my life." It's an example of your human will aligning with God's Holy Word.

Keep the word. A Rhema Word from God is special, never simply take it lightly. Pray how God might reveal it to you in your situation. The same word can apply to your life in many different situations.

Words from preachers and teachers who are anointed by God can penetrate your heart and cause you to be transformed. The engrafted word of God is able to save your soul.

James 1: 21 Therefore lay aside all filthiness and remaining wickedness and receive with meekness the engrafted word, which is able to save your souls.

22 Be doers of the word and not hearers only, deceiving yourselves. 23 For if anyone is a hearer of the word and not a doer, he is like a man viewing his natural face in a mirror. 24 He views himself, and goes his way, and immediately forgets what kind of man he was. 25 But whoever looks into the perfect law of liberty, and continues in it, and is not a forgetful hearer but a doer of the work, this man will be blessed in his deeds.

Apply the Word in your life. Pray that God would show you areas of your life to apply the revelation. Pray for it in all areas of authority in your life. Obey the Word of God so that your life aligns with it completely. The Word of God is not just a book. It is God's living will concerning you. God's words are spirit and life. They can change your spirit, soul, body.

God's Words are life

John 6: 63 It is the Spirit who gives life. The flesh profits nothing. The words that I speak to you are spirit and are life.

Ask the Holy Spirit to be with you helping you throughout your day. Keep in a posture of prayer meaning be quick to pray. Always give thanks for the answer.

Be willing and obedient

Be a willing vessel. Offer yourself to God each day. Be obedient to the word of God and the promptings of God. Enjoy living with God. His Holy presence brings peace, joy, prosperity, strength. God created you to have intimate communion with Himself. Enjoy His presence in prayer, praise, worship and studying the word of God.

Revelation 4: 1 "You are worthy, O Lord,
   to receive glory and honor and power;
for You have created all things,
   and by Your will they exist
   and were created."

Be a joyful servant.

    Should you have the joy of communion with God, start sharing with others. Let others know how much God loves them. Offer yourself to serve whether it be speaking to someone or a small group or a large group. Expect the Holy Spirit to use you. Offer yourself to serve by greeting people with sincere compassion and caring. Use all aspects of your everyday life to affect the people within your life so that the love of Christ shines from within you.

Psalm 100: 2 Serve the Lord with gladness;
   come before His presence with singing.
3 Know that the Lord, He is God;
   it is He who has made us, and not we ourselves;
   we are His people, and the sheep of His pasture.

    Pray with confidence knowing God hears you. Begin to pray for others knowing it changes things as angels are released to bring the word into being.

1 John 5: 14 This is the confidence that we have in Him, that if we ask anything according to His will, He hears us. 15 So if we know that He hears whatever we ask, we know that we have whatever we asked of Him.

    Whatever you do, always seek God in faith believing that He is and that He is a rewarder of those who diligently seek him. Stir up your faith. Literally pray over yourself and say "I stir up my faith." Doing it releases faith in you. Do it often. Do it daily.

Hebrews 11: 6 And without faith it is impossible to please God, for he who comes to God must believe that He exists and that He is a rewarder of those who diligently seek Him.

Consecrate yourself spirit, soul and body to live for God. Give yourself wholly unto God: spirit, soul and body. Offer yourself to God as a vessel He can use: expect The Holy Spirit to lead you, prompt you and use you.

1 Thessalonians 5: 23 May the very God of peace sanctify you completely. And I pray to God that your whole spirit, soul, and body be preserved blameless unto the coming of our Lord Jesus Christ. 24 Faithful is He who calls you, who also will do it.

SAMPLE PRAYER Consecration to the Holy Spirit

Holy Spirit,

Thank you that you live in me. You are my teacher, my helper. You give me understanding and revelation. Let my life align with the Word of God. Holy Spirit, let my words align with the word of God. Correct me if I am in error. Holy Spirit, I give myself to your leading so that you can direct my steps and my paths. Quicken the scriptures to me. Give me wisdom from above that is pure and without guile. Give me a humble, gentle spirit. Let the word of God be engrafted into my very soul until I become as a living epistle. Use my life to magnify Jesus. Use my life to magnify Jehovah. Holy Spirit use me to share Christ with others. Prompt me to pray. Use me to give, to serve and to encourage all the days of my life.
In Jesus name,
Amen.

Aspects to consider

1. Write a list of prominent words God has spoken to your life. Should they include scriptures write the scriptures – yes of course you could type them but don't stop there. Print them so that you will be able to say them and pray them.
2. Write a list of prayer topics – create or reorganize your prayer list. If you have not prayed for any of the areas mentioned in this book, please add at least one area to your prayer life.
3. Keep a journal of things God is speaking to you. If possible write it on a card or on a digital device so you can see it daily and review and consider the things God is speaking to you.
4. Describe your calling in terms of what people you can reach with God's light. It includes evangelism but also includes family, friends and associates. Document the difference in your calling within different spheres such as the following:

Family, Church, Education, Health Care, Technology, Media, Business, Arts, Entertainment, Government or leadership

5. Consider how you can best reach others with the light that God has given you: prayer, friendships, one on one, small groups or large groups. Begin to write your goals and dreams of what you would do to share Christ's light with others.

PRAYERS

PRAYERS

The following prayers are samples of prayers you could pray for important reasons. You could pray the same meaning in your own words. The prayers are meant as examples only.

PRAYER To yield to The Holy Spirit

Holy Spirit, I give myself to you, spirit, soul body. Use me. I desire to do the will of God. Speak to me. Quicken scriptures to me. Use me in the gifts of the spirit. Use me to build up, to encourage, to teach, to shine the way to Jesus Christ. Amen.

PRAYER FOR SALVATION

Thank you- Jesus that you died for me on the cross. Thank you that you rose from the dead and ascended into heaven. Thank you that you are coming back again. I thank you Jesus for forgiving my sins. Thank you for your blood that cleanses me from all sin and unrighteousness. Thank you that your blood makes me holy. Thank you for saving me. Fill me with the Holy Spirit to overflowing. I pray for the baptism of the Holy Spirit. Lead me to other people who love you and serve you and that can help me know more about you. Give me the discerning of spirits strong. I thank you and praise you. With my mouth, I confess Jesus Christ is my LORD. Amen.

PRAYER FOR BAPTISM OF THE HOLY SPIRIT

Thank you- Jesus that you promised to send the gift of the Holy Spirit to us. Thank you that this promise is to all believers. I am a believer. I want all of you that you will give me. I want to know you God. Baptize me in the Holy Spirit with the evidence of speaking in other tongues. I believe you want to fill me to overflowing with your Spirit so that I might be an effective witness for Christ on the earth. Thank you for saving me. Thank you for your Holy presence. [begin praising God for what He has done for you – sing worship choruses and praise God in your natural language. Believe that He is present with you – start praising and worshipping Him. As phrases come to you in other tongues, say them – praise God with new tongues.] I praise you. I thank you. I receive the baptism of the Holy Spirit.

PRAYER FOR RELEASING ANGELS

God, I thank you that angels are ministering spirits sent as ministers to us. I pray over my prayer request NAME IT HERE. God I pray release angels to perform it. I thank you for releasing the answer to me. I praise you for it. Amen.

PRAYER FOR RESISTING EVIL

I am the redeemed of the LORD. Jesus Christ has saved me. I am a new creation in Christ Jesus. Jesus blood covers me. I live in the spirit. The Holy Spirit of God fills my spirit. O Holy Spirit quicken me; give me wisdom. Pray [expecting God will give you discerning of spirits so you will have the right words to speak.]

In the name of Jesus Christ, I bind you. I rebuke you evil spirit. In the name of Jesus, I command you to go out. You have no place in my life. I cast you out. You have no place with me. I am covered by the blood of Jesus and His righteousness is my righteousness. Go out evil spirit in the name of Jesus Christ!

Thank you, Holy Spirit for your holy presence. Release angels to drive out the enemy. Thank you. Amen.

PRAYER FOR PROTECTION

Holy Spirit release angels to protect me. I plead the blood of Jesus over me. I pray the protection you promise to your people. Cover me Jesus. Holy Spirit give me wisdom, discernment and understanding. Thank you for angels that guard over me. Thank you for your blood that protects me and a hedge of protection around me. I praise you O God. [praise God with some worship choruses and expect God's holy presence to be manifest in you]. Thank you. O God for protection.

PRAYER FOR HEALING

Lord Jesus, Thank you that you gave your life for me so that I can be saved, healed and delivered. I thank you for the scripture that by your stripes I am healed. I thank you for my healing.

NAME THE DISEASE I bind you in the name of Jesus. I cast you out. I pray over myself that I would be whole spirit, soul and body.

Thank you, God. for your healing manifestation in my life. I give you all the glory. Amen.

PRAYER OF REPENTENCE

Jesus, thank you for your blood shed for me. I repent of the sin of NAME IT. I thank you for liberty from sin. I cut off the root of iniquity in my family. I thank you for your empowering presence to live a Holy life. Holy Spirit lead and guide me in the paths of righteousness. Thank you for giving me godly desires. Let my life align with your word. In Jesus name. Amen.

Prayer of dedication as a giver

God, thank you for prospering me. Let me be a giver you can use to give to others. God let my character be humble and giving so that you place things and wealth in my hands and I will give as you lead me. If you prosper me with more than enough, I will obey your promptings to give to the gospel, to people and for the glory of God. Use me as a giver. I give myself wholly to you. In Jesus name. Amen.

Prayer for deliverance

Jesus, I thank you I can speak with you my Saviour and my LORD. I renounce sin and the addiction of NAME IT. Your word says that who you set free stays free in Jesus. I need you to help me. I plead your blood over me. In the name of Jesus I rebuke you sin of NAME IT. You have no place in me! My body is a temple of the Holy Spirit. Holy Spirit teach me and quicken the scriptures to me so that I may live in the spirit.

Jesus, By faith I ask you to connect me with strong believing Christians who can help me to live a holy life. Thank you. Amen.

OTHER BOOKS BY CHRIS A. LEGEBOW

Available on Amazon.ca Amazon.com or Kindle
Or the Create Space webstore.

By Living Word Publishers

Angels: Ministering Spirits

An Excellent Spirit: Living Life Wholly Unto God

Covenant With God: God's Relationship With Man

Discipling the Generation

Discovering and Using your Spiritual Gifts

Divine Healing in the Scriptures: God's Mercy Towards Man

Jesus Christ: Saviour, Healer, Deliverer, LORD

Kinds of Giving: From the Holy Scriptures

Signs of Jesus Coming

Spheres of Authority: Know yours

The Commandments

The Doctrine of Christ: Essential Truths of Scripture

Continued…

OTHER BOOKS BY CHRIS A. LEGEBOW

The Five-Fold Ministry: Gifts to the Church

Kinds of Prayer. Knowing Them and Using Them Effectively

Living Life Fully: Knowing your Purpose

The Anointing: the Glory of God

The High Calling: Life Worth Living

The Sacraments: A Charismatic Guide

ABOUT THE AUTHOR

Chris Legebow is a Christian Professor of English and Communications. She has taught at the elementary, high school and College and University levels. She has ministered in her local churches in intercessory prayer, teaching Sunday school and other Christian Doctrine classes to children and youth. She has preached to congregations and given her testimony. Although she was not raised in a Christian home, she came to know Jesus Christ as her Saviour and LORD while she was studying in University. This radically transformed her life in terms of priorities and commitment.

She has a strong passion for the great commission – that Jesus Christ would be preached throughout all the earth believing that it a major sign of the LORD's return. She has been a part of several different types of full gospel charismatic churches but has also gained much of her insight and enlightenment from Christian Media and broadcasting. She hopes to continue ministering, serving, interceding and giving and teaching until the LORD returns.

www.ingramcontent.com/pod-product-compliance
Lightning Source LLC
Chambersburg PA
CBHW032134040426
42449CB00005B/242